Spanish
Problem
Solver

Date: 1/8/21

PRACTICE MAKES PERFECT™

Spanish Problem Solver

Eric W. Vogt, Ph.D.

New York Chicago San Francisco Lisbon London Madrid Mexico City
Milan New Delhi San Juan Seoul Singapore Sydney Toronto

The McGraw-Hill Companies

Copyright © 2012 by The McGraw-Hill Companies, Inc. All rights reserved. Printed in the United States of America. Except as permitted under the United States Copyright Act of 1976, no part of this publication may be reproduced or distributed in any form or by any means, or stored in a database or retrieval system, without the prior written permission of the publisher.

2 3 4 5 6 7 8 9 10 11 12 13 14 15   QDB/QDB   1 9 8 7 6 5 4 3 2

ISBN: 978-0-07-175619-8

Library of Congress Control Number 2011928667

Trademarks: McGraw-Hill, the McGraw-Hill Publishing logo, Practice Makes Perfect, and related trade dress are trademarks or registered trademarks of The McGraw-Hill Companies and/or its affiliates in the United States and other countries and may not be used without written permission. All other trademarks are the property of their respective owners. The McGraw-Hill Companies is not associated with any product or vendor mentioned in this book.

McGraw-Hill books are available at special quantity discounts to use as premiums and sales promotions or for use in corporate training programs. To contact a representative, please e-mail us at bulksales@mcgraw-hill.com.

This book is printed on acid-free paper.

This volume is dedicated to all learners and lovers of the Spanish language,
whithersoever dispersed around the globe.

Contents

Preface

Practice Makes Perfect: Spanish Problem Solver is both a reference work and a workbook for intermediate students who are working toward mastery of the Spanish language. You, as an intermediate student, have been engaged with the material and are laboring to get a lot of information about vocabulary, grammar rules, and pronunciation classified, understood—and ready for use on the tip of your tongue. Intermediate students can feel the weight of what they are learning grow, even as the job of learning more *must* go on. This is a critical period for you. You may struggle with patterned errors which, if not corrected, become fossilized and difficult to unlearn. Indeed, being a successful learner depends a great deal on seeking patterns, and this requires paying attention to detail as well as to the big picture. Unfortunately, too many intermediate students decide that there is just too much to learn, and give up—just when they could have found a book like this one to straighten out the major tangles in their minds and give them courage to move on.

The problems addressed in this book are not the only ones that intermediate learners will have. However, the book does attempt to cover the most common problems, the ones that I, as a teacher and professional translator of this beautiful language for thirty years, have seen intermediate students struggle with. Over the years, I've assembled an arsenal of ideas and examples to help students see these problems from different angles. Thus, it gives me pleasure and professional pride to believe that my success as a teacher of Spanish is what has led McGraw-Hill to invite me to write this book for you.

This book should sit alongside your grammars, dictionaries, and the other Spanish language materials you consult when preparing an oral presentation, a written report, or when studying for any grammar test. It is also a workbook, and yet, while there are exercises to reinforce the lessons, accompanied by explanatory answer keys, there is no need to proceed through the book in any particular sequence. After all, no rule is more important than another. If your goal is to speak Spanish correctly, then all rules are important. All the chapters, which are intended as advice and guidance about how to make your learning of Spanish more efficient and enjoyable, are accompanied by exercises. The keys to the exercises also provide explanations in cases where the correct answer given (or even wrong answers chosen) might not be immediately apparent when checking your work.

Finally, you certainly will not find answers to all your questions here, and that is as it must be, for the topics here are finite in number when compared with the vastness, depth, and richness of the Spanish language. Be assured that as you begin your study of this volume, it is my deepest hope that, partly because of my efforts at this stage of your study of Spanish, you eventually will not need it any more.

Acknowledgments

I wish to express my deepest gratitude to my Chicago editor, Garret Lemoi, of McGraw-Hill, for his years of constant encouragement and support. This, my fifth volume in their Practice Makes Perfect series, like the others, would never have seen the light of day without his unwavering confidence in my labors.

Also, my sincerest admiration and thanks go to Ms. Lylje Klein, a native of Venezuela, who for nearly ten years has generously been a second pair of eyes for nearly every scholarly article or book I have written. She has conscientiously proofed my work, ranging from my manuscripts and translations of five volumes of Spanish Baroque lyrics by the Spanish Carmelite composer Cristóbal Galán and their preliminary studies, to articles on more modern literary themes, including criticism on Gabriel García Márquez's *Cien años de soledad* and Rudyard Kipling's curious poem, *The Palace* (1902). Ms. Klein's lively and perceptive criticism and advice over the years never missed a detail in either English or Spanish. Yet, if there be faults, they remain mine.

My sincerest thanks also go to Ms. Roxanna Soto for her many years of enthusiastic use and endorsement of my books in this series and for ideas of what to include in this one. Her praise for them has encouraged me by letting me know they are making a difference for students.

Last but never least, my warmest thanks to Jacqueline Joy Sanderson of Nikao, Rarotonga, Cook Islands, New Zealand. It has been a pleasure and a privilege to consult with her regularly over the Internet and occasionally over the phone. A retired professor of English who taught with distinction for nine years at Collegiate and Raumati College in New Zealand and the prestigious Christ's College in the Cook Islands, and for fifteen years at Nukutere College in Rarotonga, her elegant explanations of English modal and phrasal verbs, history, morphology, and usage of English pronouns and forms of address are as informative as they are charming to hear or delightful to read. She is an inspiring ornament to Her Majesty's English. Her perspectives enlightened my ability to contrast English and Spanish.

To my family, I offer the warmest hope that all the time I've spent with these books and so many other necessary worldly pursuits can be made up and with interest.

Spelling and pronunciation

This chapter will show you how to reconcile written and spoken Spanish words so you can understand and read them aloud with accuracy. Students are sometimes confused about the rules and mechanics of writing in Spanish, which makes their written work difficult to follow. Since pre-college education includes less and less attention to grammatical issues, most students are adrift in misty confusion because they don't know how to name what they are confused about. This chapter, therefore, also contains some observations about the parts of speech and a bit of basic grammar terminology.

Accent marks and pronunciation

Spanish slowly emerged as a written language, consciously and clearly distinct from Latin, during the late Middle Ages. There were no rules, no one to guide its development. Most people were illiterate. English was in a similar condition when it emerged from the amalgam of languages that contributed to its development.

In 1728, more than one hundred years after the death of Cervantes, the Royal Academy of the Spanish Language was founded, and still exists today, to watch over the language and safeguard its transmission to future generations. (English has no such body, and this explains in part why there are so many differences in spelling throughout the English-speaking world.)

Some of the important features of Spanish spelling, known more formally as *orthography*, are that the Academy eventually dropped double consonants, such as *ss* and *tt* and simplified *ph* to *f* and *th* to *t*. Words with a *cc* in the middle are not considered a consonant pair because the first *c* ends the previous syllable and the second *c* begins the next, such as in **diccionario**. The famous double or trilled **rr**, as in **perro** (*dog*) as opposed to **pero** (*but*), actually represents a different sound and can be considered as if it were one letter. The good news here is that many English words are cognates with Spanish and only require you to understand a handful of rules in order to spell—and thus pronounce— them correctly. One example is sufficient to make this point. The English word *commission* is **comisión** in Spanish.

The only other small detail in this example has to do with the use of written accent marks. Over time, the Academy established more and more conservative rules about accent marks. There are four rules, and they can actually help you learn to pronounce words even if you've never seen or heard them before. Here's how the system works:

1

- Observing that a vast number of the words in Spanish end in a vowel, an **-n**, or an **-s**, and that these words are almost always pronounced by stressing the next-to-the-last syllable, the Royal Academy economically ruled that such words would not bear a written accent. What this means to you, as a learner of Spanish, is that when you see a word of more than one syllable, with no written accent and that ends in a vowel, an **-n**, or an **-s**, you should immediately know to pronounce it with the stress on the next-to-the-last syllable. It really is that simple. Open any dictionary, or **diccionario**.

- The Academy also noticed that the second largest number of words in Spanish end in a consonant other than **-n** or **-s** and that they are pronounced with the stress on the last syllable. They decided that these words also would not bear a written accent. All infinitives are examples of such words, as are all those ending in **-dad** or **-tud** (which are also, by the way, all feminine in gender). Other common examples include **animal**, stressed on the final **-a**, and **reloj**, stressed on the final **-o**.

- The next observation of the Royal Academy results in the third rule and is very important: all exceptions to the first two rules will be marked by a written accent. Remember, the exceptions are determined by how words are pronounced, speech being prior to any written system. Thus, we have many, many words ending in **-ión** (almost all feminine), such as **comisión** and **nación**, as well as others such as **fármaco, malévolo**, and **cónsul**. The point is, if you know these three rules and see a word in print, you should be able to correctly put the stress on the proper syllable of a Spanish word, even if you've never seen or heard the word before.

- The fourth and last rule about the use of written accents applies only to a means of distinguishing between two otherwise identical one-syllable words. These are known as *monosyllabic homonyms*, one-syllable words that sound alike but have different meanings. Examples of contrastive pairs include **tú** (*you*) and **tu** (*your*), **él** (*he*) and **el** (*the*, masculine singular) **té** (*tea*) and **te** (object pronoun corresponding to **tú**) **sé** (*I know*) and **se** (the third-person object pronoun).

Finally, there is only one group of words that stand outside these rules and cause difficulty. In English these words end in *-cy* and in Spanish they end in **-ia** or **-ía**. There is simply no way to predict whether they will be stressed on the final **i** or on the next-to-the-last syllable. The best strategy is to look them up—and pay attention as you read. Examples include **farmacia, malicia, farmacología**, and **alevosía**. You're in luck, of course, if you first encounter such words in print, since the presence or lack of a written accent will tell you where to place the stress when pronouncing them.

Pronunciation

A couple of general remarks may help you improve your Spanish pronunciation and make it closer to that of native speakers. First, vowels are pure. That means, for instance, that the (American) English vowel sounds as heard in cat, set, sit, on, and up are not found in Spanish—ever! Instead, the Spanish pronunciation of these vowels is more like those heard in the following (American) English words:

a *father*
e *weigh*
i *seen*
o *woe*
u *moon*

It only takes a slight adjustment to these to get them right: The sound of the **e** should not glide up into the *i* sound in *weigh* or the *y* sound in *they*. Likewise, the pronunciation of **u** in Spanish, represented approximately by the *oo* in *moon*, should not glide into an *ee* sound at the end or glide from it at the beginning, as is sometimes heard in some dialects of U.S. English. I've heard this phenomenon most often in Western states, particularly in Southern California. Even Ronald Reagan's pronunciation had a touch of this!

Regarding consonants, the best advice I can give you here is to soften them. English speakers everywhere tend to explode the pronunciation of initial occlusive consonants in particular, such as are heard in *Carl*, *Tom*, and *Peter*. One way to practice this is to hold the back of your hand about an inch away from the your lips and practice saying these names in a normal volume and pitch, but without so much force, so that you no longer feel your breath on the back of your hand.

The next and last bit of guidance I offer about pronunciation is to listen and read much. But to whom should you listen and what should you read? The choice is yours, of course, but my advice is to remember that you will be judged by how you speak—in socio-economic and class terms. True, your Spanish-speaking listeners will realize that you are not a native speaker, but they will judge you anyway, because the way you speak will suggest to them the sort of company you keep. As the Spanish proverb goes: **Dime con quién andas y te diré quién eres.** (Literally, *Tell me with who you hang out with and I'll tell you who you are.*) For speech models, I often suggest that learners judiciously follow a character from a **telenovela** (*soap opera*) who is about their age and gender and who represents a respectable character. I've known more than one native speaker of Spanish who vastly improved his or her English by doing the same thing with American "soaps."

The one remaining question I often hear from forward-looking learners who may have specific career goals that could lead them in specific geographical directions is which dialect of Spanish they should emulate. Depending on how you define them, in simple, practical terms there are six or seven major dialectical regions in the Spanish-speaking world. Each, of course, can be further subdivided, but for my readers, as learners of Spanish, the contours I shall present will enable you to make some informed decisions about the dialect you select as your model.

In Spain, there are those who pronounce the letter **z** and the consonant-vowel combinations **ce-/ci-** as the *th* sound of the English word *thin* (often called *theta*, after the name of the Greek letter). There are others who do not follow this pattern and who pronounce these sounds approximately as an *s*. The dividing line is roughly north-south, the north being the zone of the *theta* pronunciation. The ancestors of most of the people of the New World were from the south of Spain, which largely explains why the pronunciation of Castile is not found in the Americas.

In the Americas, the major dialect groups are: Mexican, Caribbean (Cuba, Dominican Republic, Puerto Rico and coastal areas of Central America, Colombia and Venezuela), Central American (except Caribbean coastal areas), Andean (interior of Colombia, Peru, Ecuador, most of Chile, Bolivia and Paraguay), and finally the area known as the **Cono del Sur** or Southern Cone (Argentina, southern Chile, and Uruguay).

Spanish in the United States itself is evolving. In South Florida, New York, and New Jersey, you will find mostly Caribbean dialects. In Chicago, Minneapolis–St. Paul, and other Midwestern cities, as well as in most of the Western states, the Mexican dialect predominates. Interestingly, in the metropolitan area of Washington, D.C., the Salvadoran dialect predominates, due to the presence of more than a hundred thousand immigrants who fled El Salvador in the 1980s.

No one dialect is superior to another. The Royal Academy has corresponding members in every corner of the world where Spanish is or ever has been a language of government. There are educated and non-educated speakers in each dialect, so if you have professional reasons for spending much time in any particular region, you should seek out people of your profession who are from there so you can fit in as easily as possible. This book, therefore, takes a neutral approach in its choice of vocabulary, a sort of *airport* dialect, if you wish.

The brief set of exercises that follow give practice in the use of the dictionary—to check spellings, accent marks, and proper classification according to part of speech. It is assumed that learners will also be pronouncing the words they find.

EJERCICIO
1·1

Indicate whether the following words correctly use accent marks or do not require one according to the following key: **correctly used***;* **incorrectly placed** *(but needed on a different syllable);* **correct, with no accent mark***;* **superfluous** *(placed on syllable that would be stressed anyway); or* **missing.**

1. organizacion _____

2. consul _____

3. lealtad _____

4. animál _____

5. camión _____

6. tecnologia _____

7. háblas _____

8. teorico _____

9. temeraria _____

10. primorosa _____

11. caracter _____

12. avíon _____

13. caracteres _____

14. vendio _____

15. ventána _____

16. vecino _____

17. frijoles _____

18. proyector _____

19. cortinas _____

20. teoría _____

Forms of address, statements and questions, and social conventions

The best and most traditional place to begin when introducing the topic of forms of address is with the well-known distinction of the use of the two singular forms of address, **tú** and **usted**, commonly abbreviated **Ud.**, and sometimes as **Vd**. As you already know, the use of the **tú** form is reserved for family and friends in most places in the Spanish-speaking world.

In terms of its cultural usage, this distinction is a big deal in many places. While we in the United States tend to throw the word *friend* around rather loosely, for most Latinos, **amigo** or **amiga** is generally taken more seriously, and thus the **tú** form is reserved for people who truly are special. I have heard people being rebuked for using the **tú** form without really knowing the person. Use **Ud.** until you are given permission, or you are invited to use the **tú** form (you'll probably be told **tutéame, por favor**—meaning *use the tú form with me, please*). The only exception is that among young people, **tú** tends to be used automatically, but these same young people likely would not dare to use it when speaking to strangers who are older.

Most students have no problem with the concept of having a polite and a familiar form of address. Using **tú** is somewhat comparable to being on a first-name basis with someone, while using **usted** is more like using Mr. or Ms. in the English-speaking world.

Many students encounter a stumbling block when they first encounter **tú** and **usted** and any residual confusion often continues into the intermediate level, resulting in imperfect mastery of the verb forms and even patterned errors. Part of the problem is that **usted** and **ustedes** are *second-person in meaning but require the third-person forms of verbs*. Let's examine this problem in more detail.

The personal pronoun **usted** is derived from **Vuestra Merced**, meaning *Your Mercy* or *Your Grace*, which, because it is an indirect way of speaking to someone, requires the third-person form of verbs.

There are four ways to say *you* in Spanish: formal and familiar, singular and plural, and all refer to a second-person. Keep in mind that the second person is defined as the person or persons *to whom* one is speaking when that person is the subject of a statement or question. The two singular forms are **tú** and **usted**; the two plural forms are **vosotros** and **ustedes**. **Vosotros** is used almost exclusively in Spain and is simply the plural of the familiar **tú** with its corresponding verb form. In the Americas, **ustedes** is used for any situation when the plural of *you* is used, a fact that comes as a bit of relief for English-speaking students of Spanish.

7

If the same statement or question is expressed using any of the other Spanish forms of *you*, the English "translation" remains the same. However, keep in mind that the verb form changes, since it must agree with the subject in person and number. Observe these examples in which all the other forms of *you* are used. Note also that the following sentences and questions are great examples of how "translation" requires more than the mere rendering of words. For our immediate purposes, however, two things should be noted in comparing them. First, the parentheses indicate the subject pronoun the speaker has in mind. Secondly, since there is no other subject associated with the **tú** and the **vosotros** form of verbs, this pronoun would not need to be used; however, since **usted** and **ustedes** employ the third-person form of the verb, these subject pronouns might need to be used in order to avoid misunderstanding:

(Tú) **estudias** por la tarde.	*You study in the afternoon.*
¿**Estudias** (tú) por la tarde?	*Do you study in the afternoon?*
(Usted) **estudia** por la tarde.	*You study in the afternoon.*
¿**Estudia** (usted) por la tarde?	*Do you study in the afternoon?*
Estudiáis por la tarde.	*You study in the afternoon.*
¿**Estudiáis** por la tarde?	*Do you study in the afternoon?*
(Ustedes) **estudian** por la tarde.	*You study in the afternoon.*
¿**Estudian** (ustedes) por la tarde?	*Do you study in the afternoon?*

EJERCICIO
2·1

Indicate how you should address the following people as either **tú**, **Ud.**, **vosotros**, *or* **Uds.**, *according to the situation described.*

1. A un juez, que es su amigo, en un tribunal de justicia. _____

2. Al mismo juez, que es su amigo, en una fiesta familiar. _____

3. A su tío. _____

4. A un desconocido, mayor de edad, en la calle. _____

5. A dos niños, en España. _____

6. A tres personas, en Latinoamérica. _____

7. A sus abuelos, en España. _____

8. A las amigas de sus padres, a quienes Ud. no conoce. _____

9. A un compañero de clase. _____

10. A unas compañeras de clase, en España. _____

Select the sentence or question with the correct form of address and correspondingly proper verb form, according to the situational cues.

1. A un amigo, en una fiesta.

   a. ¿Cómo está usted, Tomás?

   b. Me gustan tus zapatos.

   c. ¡Qué elegantes son!

2. A un profesor, en la clase.

   a. ¿Le puedo hacer una pregunta, señor?

   b. ¿Nos vas a dar un examen mañana?

   c. ¿Qué hacen Uds. este fin de semana?

3. A varios amigos, en una fiesta en Madrid.

   a. Espero que puedan venir a casa este fin de semana.

   b. ¿Queréis tomar una copa conmigo en el balcón?

   c. ¿Han visto a Jaime?

4. Al público, en una conferencia.

   a. El discurso que voy a presentarles...

   b. El discurso que voy a presentarte...

   c. El discurso que voy a presentaros...

5. A su padre.

   a. ¿Quiere ir a pescar este fin de semana?

   b. ¿Quieres jugar al tenis esta tarde?

   c. ¿Desean ir a la playa mañana?

6. A varios jugadores en su equipo de fútbol, en Málaga.

   a. Pasan la pelota muy despacio.

   b. Tienes que correr un kilómetro o dos todos los días.

   c. Podéis ganar si practicáis más.

7. A sus compañeros de trabajo, en Latinoamérica.

   a. El jefe quiere hablar con Ud.

   b. ¿No van a participar en la conferencia la semana que viene?

   c. No me habléis de asuntos personales, por favor.

8. A una cajera, en el banco, a quien no conoce.

   a. ¿Podría darme un sobre para este cheque?

   b. Dame un sobre en el que pueda guardar este cheque.

   c. Espero que tengáis un sobre para este cheque.

9. A sus profesores.

   a. Yo los admiro mucho por lo que me han enseñado.

   b. Quiero felicitarte por la publicación de tantos artículos.

   c. ¿Tenéis tiempo disponible para explicar las notas que me habéis dado?

10. A su mamá y su hermana gemela, en Sevilla.

    a. Su cumpleaños es este fin de semana. ¡Qué emoción!

    b. Quiero daros una fiesta de cumpleaños.

    c. ¿No vienen con sus primas?

11. A su hermano.

    a. ¿No oye lo que dice en la radio?

    b. Si tienen sed, tomen agua.

    c. Oye, ¡no me pidas dinero todo el tiempo!

12. A su padre y un tío, en España.

    a. ¿No podéis acompañarme a comer unas tapas?

    b. Sé que desean ir a Pamplona este verano.

    c. Préstenme unos euros para que pueda comprar un coche.

13. A su nuevo jefe, mayor de edad, en México.

    a. Gracias por la oficina tan amplia que me dio.

    b. Son muy amables por haberme contratado.

    c. ¿Deseáis ir a ver una película esta noche?

14. Una mamá, en una consulta con el pediatra.

    a. Por favor, quiero que me dé una receta para quitarle el dolor a mi bebe.

    b. ¿Qué me recomiendan para bajarle la fiebre a mi bebé?

    c. ¿Crees que mi bebé tiene la gripe?

15. Un esposo a su esposa.

    a. ¡Dame un besito, mi amor!

    b. ¿Quiere ver la tele o prefiere salir a dar un paseo?

    c. Le doy cien dólares para comprar un nuevo suéter.

Articles

English has only one definite article (*the*) and two indefinite articles (*a* and *an*). Since Spanish has four of each, due to gender and number (as pointed out in the introduction), their usage is not entirely identical to English. In some cases, the usage differs considerably. This chapter will examine articles and help you correct or avoid many errors typical of English speakers.

Inextricably linked to the topic of articles is the topic of grammatical gender. For English speakers, gender tends to be either a scientific or a political topic, not a grammatical issue. Thus, in English, gender only tends to be applied to living things that have gender: many animal species, just as in words referring to people, have distinct words for the male and female, for instance: man, woman, boy, girl, bull, cow, ram, ewe, rooster, hen. In other words, the English language bases all considerations of gender on the nature of the noun in question. Only in poetry or older forms of speech does one read or hear, for instance, a ship being called "she." By the way, English is the only European language without gender, which is one reason English speakers have a difficult time learning the other ones.

First of all, let's face the fact that grammatical gender makes no sense. There is nothing logical about why the word **silla** (*chair*) should be feminine while **escritorio** (*desk*) should be masculine. At best, an appeal to the history of languages can only offer descriptions and tell us what happened, but it cannot solve the problem of why gender has been assigned to nouns.

Another fact is that, except for nouns that can apply equally to a male or female, such as **artista** (*artist*), and whose gender is marked by the article used, a noun's gender is invariable. It does not depend on, nor is it affected by, the gender of the speaker or owner. Many intermediate students will mistakenly assign their own gender to nouns, especially when speaking of things they own. Thus, if a woman wears **pantalones** (*pants*), they are still grammatically masculine (and, as in English, always plural). Likewise, even if a man wears a **camisa** (*shirt*) the word **camisa** is still feminine. The arbitrariness of the gender of nouns is a thorn in the side for many English speaking learners of Spanish, but it need not be. Let's get the big picture and then go into specifics.

Most Spanish nouns end in either an unstressed **-a** or an unstressed **-o**. Those ending in **-a** are mostly feminine. Those ending in **-o** are mostly masculine. Exceptions include **la mano** (*the hand*) and **el día** (*the day* or *the morning*). Other exceptions are words derived from Greek that end in **-ma**, **-pa**, or **-ta**. There are only a few, but they are high-frequency vocabulary items and are all cognate with English—**el problema**, **el tema**, **el drama**, **el programa**, **el mapa**, and **el planeta**—and are all masculine.

Spanish nouns that begin with a stressed **a** (whether or not the accent is written) and end in **a** are truly feminine, but when they are singular, you need to use the masculine singular article. Examples: **el hacha** (*the axe*) but **las hachas** (*the* *axes*). Likewise, **el águila** (*the eagle*) forms its plural as **las águilas** (*the eagles*), and **el agua** (*the water*) becomes **las aguas** (*the waters*). Notwithstanding this rule, these words are truly feminine and thus, when modified by an adjective, that adjective must always be feminine, whether the word is used in the singular or plural: **el agua fría** and **las aguas frías**.

As touched upon in the introduction, Spanish nouns ending in **-ción, -sión, -dad**, and **-tud** are all feminine and often are cognate with English words that end in **-tion, -ty**, and **-tude**. Not all words ending in **-ión,** however are feminine. Three common words— **gorrión, avión**, and **camión**—are masculine and mean, respectively, *sparrow, airplane*, and *truck*. Also feminine are words ending in **-umbre**, such as **costumbre, lumbre, mansedumbre, podredumbre**.

Learn the gender of nouns as you acquire vocabulary by determining their gender, then placing **el** or **la** in front of them if they are singular, and **los** or **las** in front of them if they are plural. Well conceived textbooks will have done this for you.

Remember that articles agree with the nouns they point to and that, unlike nouns, articles and adjectives not only can "morph," they must! They have to take on the gender and number of the noun they relate to.

With that in mind, you're almost ready to learn where and when not to use the articles. There are two types of articles, *definite* and *indefinite*. Their names hint at their uses, but their uses are not exactly the same as in English. The definite articles in Spanish, all of which translate as *the* are:

SINGULAR		PLURAL
Masculine	el	los
Feminine	la	las

There are only two contractions in Spanish and both involve the singular, masculine definite article **el**. Whenever the preposition **a** comes before **el**, they contract to form **al**; whenever the preposition **de** comes before **el**, they contract to form **del**. However, no contraction is formed when either of these prepositions precede the third-person, masculine singular subject pronoun **él**. In these cases, **a él** or **de él** would be written—and in speech, the **él** would be stressed slightly, without, however, a glottal stop between the words (as occurs between the words when in English we say *an apple*). No contractions are formed either when **el** or **la** is part of a proper name or even a nickname, such as **de El Salvador** (the country) or **de El Greco** (the painter).

Definite articles

The following lists of rules will help you determine how to use definite articles in Spanish. While the English definite article *the* and the Spanish definite articles **el, la, los** and **las** all are used to point out a specific noun (e.g., *the* apple as opposed to *an* apple), the use of the definite articles in Spanish differs from English in many ways:

- ◆ Use the definite article before nouns used in a general or abstract sense.

  Los caballos son inteligentes.   *Horses are intelligent.*

  Note that if one says **El caballo es inteligente**, the speaker could be referring either to a specific horse or to all horses generally, as when English uses *man* to refer to *humankind*.

  Me interesa **la poesía**.   *Poetry interests me.*
  En los hospitales se emplean **los rayos X**.   *They use X rays in hospitals.*

This rule is not always followed in book titles, but this seldom becomes an issue for English speakers. Thus *War and Peace* is known in Spanish as **Guerra y paz** (remembering, please, that the Spanish translation was done from the Russian original).

- Use the (masculine) definite article before the names of days of the week to mean *on* any given day.

El sábado vamos a la playa.	*On Saturday, we are going to the beach.*
Vamos a la playa **los sábados.**	*We go the beach on Saturdays.*

- Use the definite article before the number of the calendar day.

Es **el 26** de noviembre.	*It's November 26.*

When **hoy** is used, the definite article is omitted:

Hoy es **26** de noviembre.	*Today is November 26.*

- Use the definite article before the names of the four seasons.

Los veranos son calurosos en Sonora.	*Summers are hot in Sonora.*

Note, however, that when singling out one season to talk about events that happened then or that will happen, Spanish and English both use the indefinite article.

Un invierno en la década de los 70, no nevó nada en mi pueblo.	*One winter in the 1970s, it didn't snow in my town at all.*
Un verano de éstos, mi hija y yo vamos a viajar por todo el país en tren.	*One of these summers, my daughter and I will travel around the whole country by train.*

- Use the definite article before names of clothing and parts of the body.

Me duele **el pie.**	*My foot hurts.*
Juana se puso **el suéter** y luego salió.	*Jane put on her sweater and left.*

It also is important to remember that whereas in English, when addressing a group, the plural is used when speaking of clothing or other personal items, in Spanish the singular is used. Observe the following example:

Niños, abran **el libro.**	*Children, open your books.*

The use of the reflexive construction shows whose foot hurts and whose sweater was put on by whom.

- Use the definite article in measurements and when citing percentages.

Hoy se venden las manzanas a 50 pesos **el** (or por) **kilo.**	*Today the apples are going for 50 pesos a (or per) kilo.*
Las cebollas son a 80 pesos **la** (or por) **docena.**	*Onions are 80 pesos a (or per) dozen.*
El cinco por ciento de la población se enfermó.	*Five percent of the population fell ill.*

- Do not use the definite article before a noun in apposition (occurring when two noun phrases are placed next to each other) to another noun.

| Obama, **presidente** de los Estados Unidos, dio un discurso ante el Senado. | *Obama, the president of the United States, gave a speech before the Senate.* |
| Seattle, **puerto** principal del noroeste, llegó a ser la capital de la informática. | *Seattle, the main port in the Northwest, came to be the computer science capital.* |

The exception to this rule is when the definite article is used, as required, in a superlative construction.

| Seattle, **el tercer puerto** más grande del país, es una ciudad relativamente pequeña. | *Seattle, the third largest port in the country, is a relatively small city.* |

- Use the definite article before certain titles when speaking *about* the people who hold them.

| ¿Dónde está **el Dr. Martínez?** | *Where is Dr. Martínez?* |
| **La Sra. Gómez** es muy amable. | *Mrs. Gómez is very kind.* |

However, when speaking directly *to* someone, the definite article is *never* used before the title.

| ¡Hola, **Dr. Martínez!** | *Hi, Dr. Martínez!* |

The definite article is often used colloquially before first names; however, this practice is considered substandard.

| Oye, pero ¿no has hablado con **el Gregorio?** | *Hey, so, uh, have you talked to Greg?* |

- The definite article is never used, either when speaking of or speaking to, persons with the titles of **Don**, **Doña**, **San**, **Santo**, **Santa**, **Fray**, or **Sor**.

| **Sor Juana Inés de la Cruz** fue una mujer intelectual muy importante en México. | *Sor Juana Inés de la Cruz was a very important woman intellectual in Mexico.* |
| **Don Felipe** es un hombre muy respetado en este pueblo. | *Don Felipe is a very respected man in this town.* |

- Use the definite article when referring to a previously mentioned noun.

| No me gustó este plato, pero **el** que preparó María, sí me gustó mucho. | *I didn't like this dish, but the one María fixed, yeah, I liked it.* |
| Estas camisas son muy atractivas, no como **las** que vimos en la otra tienda. | *These shirts are very attractive, not like the ones we saw in the other store.* |

- Use the definite article in a formulaic way before the name of a group being treated collectively when expressing a collective sentiment.

Nosotros, **los mexicanos**, somos muy patriotas.	*We Mexicans are very patriotic.*
Vosotros, **los niños**, sois muy traviesos.	*You kids are very naughty.*
Nosotras, **las mujeres**, somos muy trabajadoras.	*We women are very hardworking.*

◆ Use the definite article before the names of some countries or cities.

El Canadá	El Japón	La China	La Habana
El Ecuador	El Perú	La Florida	La India

One way to remember many of these is to recall how these places were psychologically, if not geographically, remote from Spain in colonial times, and the usage stuck. Other place names, particularly countries, will never have the definite article placed before them unless they are modified, as this partial list shows.

Cuba	Francia	Italia	Rusia
España	Inglaterra	México	Suecia

However, when modified, the definite article must be used before the names of these countries.

La España del Siglo de Oro fue como Estados Unidos en el siglo XX.

Golden Age Spain was like the United States in the 20th century.

◆ Use the definite article before the names of languages, except after **en** and often after **de**, as well as after **hablar** and other verbs referring to *speaking, teaching,* and *learning* languages.

El chino es un idioma interesante.
Prefiero hablar **español.**

Chinese is an interesting language.
I prefer to speak Spanish.

But in the following example, the word **mejor** stands between **hablar** and the language, and so the definite article is used.

Estoy aprendiendo a hablar mejor **el farsi**.
Es **un libro ruso**.

I am learning to speak Farsi better.
It's a Russian book. (The book is written in Russian or published in Russia.)

Este libro es **de ruso**.

This is a Russian text. (The book is one for learning the language.)

Este artículo es **en italiano**.
Ellos aprenden **ruso**.
Lan enseña **chino**.

This article is in Italian.
They are learning Russian.
Lan teaches Chinese.

Indefinite articles

The indefinite articles in Spanish, shown here, translate as *a* and *an* for the singular forms. English, however, has no plural forms that correspond to *a* and *an*. Nevertheless, the Spanish indefinite articles do the jobs performed by *some* or *a few*.

SINGULAR		PLURAL	
Masculine	un	unos	
Feminine	una	unas	

In addition to the rule about using the masculine singular article before feminine words beginning with a stressed **a-** (or **ha-**) which also end in **-a**, the following rules should be observed about the use of the indefinite article:

◆ The indefinite article is not used before unmodified nouns referring to profession, nationality, or affiliation.

Su papá es **médico**.	*Her dad is a doctor.*
Soy **traductor**.	*I am a translator.*

However, when the noun is modified or used before a noun subject, the indefinite article must be used.

Ella es **una traductora famosa**.	*She is a famous translator.*
Un policía vino a hablarme.	*A policeman came to talk to me.*

◆ The indefinite article is omitted before **buen** or **mal** when these precede a noun.

Juan es **buen** tipo.	*John is a good guy. (More colloquially:* Juan es buena gente.*)*
Ese político es **mala** persona.	*That politician is a bad person.*

Whenever there are two descriptive adjectives modifying one noun, the simplest and most common solution is to put them both after the noun with **y** (*and*) connecting the adjectives.

Veo dos pájaros **bonitos y verdes**.	*I see two pretty, green birds.*

◆ The indefinite article is never used before the following words or expressions:

Tengo **cien** pesos.	*I have a hundred pesos.*
Cierta persona vino a verme.	*A certain person came to see me.*
Juan me ofreció **mil** excusas.	*John offered me a thousand excuses.*
Juanita nos dio **otra** explicación por lo sucedido.	*Jane gave us another explanation for what happened.*
Le di **media docena** de huevos.	*I gave him a half dozen eggs.*
¡Qué rica **la** sopa!	*What a delicious soup!*
Tal cosa no debe suceder nunca.	*Such a thing should never happen.*

However, the indefinite article is always used before **millón** (note also the use of **de** after **millón**):

Se ganó **un millón** de dólares.	*He earned a million dollars.*

◆ The indefinite article is not used after prepositions except when it means *one*, in the numerical sense.

Cuando voy al campo, voy **sin mochila**.	*When I go to the country, I go without a backpack.*
Una vez fui al campo con **una mochila** y tres cambios de ropa.	*I once went to the country with a backpack and three changes of clothes.*

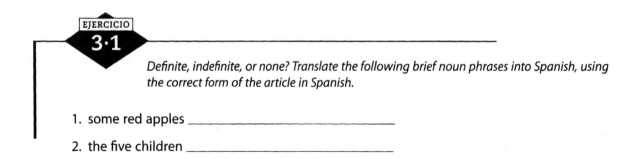

EJERCICIO
3·1

Definite, indefinite, or none? Translate the following brief noun phrases into Spanish, using the correct form of the article in Spanish.

1. some red apples _____

2. the five children _____

3. a thousand days _____

4. (speaking to) Mrs. Gómez _____

5. the many animals _____

6. a million birds _____

7. a few pencils _____

8. the tiger _____

9. another hand _____

10. the five books _____

11. the lions _____

12. (speaking of) Dr. Martínez _____

13. some watches _____

14. the palm trees _____

15. India and Japan _____

Examine the English sentences and then select the Spanish translation that properly uses (or properly does not use) the articles correctly according to the rules in Spanish. In every case, there is only one best answer.

1. One summer, we all went to the beach.

   a. Fuimos a la playa el verano pasado.

   b. Un verano, todos fuimos a la playa.

   c. Todos fuimos a la playa ese verano.

2. Today is February 12, 2011.

   a. Hoy es febrero 12 de 2011.

   b. Hoy es el 12 de febrero de 2011.

   c. Hoy es 12 de febrero de 2011.

3. Latin is one language John knows how to read.

   a. El latín es una lengua que Juan sabe leer.

   b. Latín es una lengua que Juan lee.

   c. Latín es un idioma que lee Juan.

4. Fall is the best time of the year.

    a. Otoño es la temporada más magnífica del año.

    b. La mejor temporada del año es otoño.

    c. El otoño es la mejor estación del año.

5. John's feet hurt.

    a. A Juan le duelen los pies.

    b. Sus pies le duelen a Juan.

    c. A Juan, le duelen sus pies.

6. Geometry is my favorite subject.

    a. Mi clase favorita es geometría.

    b. Mi materia favorita es la geometría.

    c. Geometría me gusta.

7. Her friends are all accountants.

    a. Sus amigos son unos contadores.

    b. Los amigos de ella son unos contadores.

    c. Todos sus amigos son contadores.

8. Mr. Acero is a bad person.

    a. Es un malo el Sr. Acero.

    b. El Sr. Acero es malo.

    c. El Sr. Acero es un malo.

9. I went to the soccer game on Sunday.

    a. Domingo, fui al partido de fútbol.

    b. Fui al partido de fútbol domingo pasado.

    c. Fui al partido de fútbol el domingo.

10. Paulina is Spanish.

    a. Paulina es la española.

    b. Paulina es una española.

    c. Paulina es española.

11. Ten percent of all those who applied were accepted.

    a. Se aceptó el diez por ciento de los solicitantes.

    b. Se aceptó el diez por ciento de todos los solicitantes.

    c. El diez por ciento de los que solicitaron fueron aceptados.

12. Did you go to Dr. Sánchez's presentation?

    a. ¿Fuiste a la presentación de Dr. Sánchez?

    b. ¿Fuiste a la presentación del Dr. Sánchez?

    c. Fuiste a la presentación de Dr. Sánchez, ¿no?

13. My friends put on their hats and left.

    a. Mis amigos se pusieron sus sombreros y salieron.

    b. Mis amigos se pusieron el sombrero y se fueron.

    c. Mis amigos se pusieron los sombreros y fueron.

14. Ms. Isabel is an elegant lady.

    a. Sra. Isabel es una señora elegante.

    b. La Srta. Isabel es una mujer elegante.

    c. Doña Isabel es una dama elegante.

15. Mr. Gómez, the head of the board of directors, decided not to speak at their meeting.

    a. El Sr. Gómez, jefe de la junta de directores, optó por no hablar en la reunión.

    b. Sr. Gómez, el jefe de la junta de directores, decidió no hablar en su reunión.

    c. El Sr. Gómez, el jefe de la junta de directores, decidió no hablar en su reunión.

Gender and number agreement

The cluster of words centered on a noun or pronoun, pointed to by a preceding article (either definite or indefinite) and then modified by an adjective (usually following the noun) is a principle building block of a sentence in Spanish. This is known as a noun phrase. The noun at the center of the cluster governs the gender and number of the words that refer to it from both sides; in other words, the words must agree with the noun, both in gender and number. Apart from its part of speech as a noun, this noun may play the grammatical role of subject or object, either direct, indirect, or as object of a preposition. This chapter focuses on how to form noun phrases, not on their grammatical function in a sentence. In this chapter you will also learn how the placement of certain adjectives either in front of or following the noun alters the the adjective to either a literal or figurative meaning.

Once you understand gender and number agreement and are comfortable with the usual word order of article, noun, and adjective, you are ready to focus on how the placement of certain adjectives makes them mean something else. In order to look at this fine-tuning closely, you need to be aware that there are two types of adjectives: descriptive and quantitative. *Descriptive adjectives*, which follow nouns, have to do with the qualities of the nouns they modify. Colors are the most obvious descriptive examples. As the name indicates, *quantitative adjectives* are those that have anything to do with number, such as **muchos** (*many, lots*), **algunos**, **unos**, or **pocos** (*some* or *a few*), and all cardinal (counting) numbers and ordinal numbers, such as **primer** or **primera** (*first*), **segundo**, **segunda** (*second*), and so on. The following example shows both a qualitative and a quantitative adjective in action and modifying the same noun:

Hay **muchas** flores **rojas** aquí. *There are many red flowers here.*

One comment about **primer**: its full form is **primero** (in the masculine) but it always drops the final **-o** before a singular masculine noun. The feminine form, **primera**, does not shorten, regardless of its position relative to the noun it modifies.

Según la leyenda bíblica, el *According to the biblical account,*
  primer hombre fue Adán. *the first man was Adam.*
Casi nadie se acuerda del *Almost no one knows the name*
  nombre del **tercer** hombre *of the third man who went to*
  que fue a la luna. *the moon.*

The general rule for the placement of adjectives is that descriptive adjectives follow nouns and quantitative adjectives precede them.

Su mamá preparó **una cena sabrosa**.	*His mom fixed a delicious dinner.*
Arlena es **una mujer extraordinaria**.	*Arlene is an extraordinary woman.*
Vi **tres gatos** en el callejón anoche.	*I saw three cats in the alley last night.*
Había **varios muchachos** jugando al fútbol en el parque ayer.	*There were a few guys playing soccer in the park yesterday.*

There are two types of descriptive adjectives that must always follow nouns: adjectives of nationality and any adjective modified by an adverb, such as **muy** (*very*).

Ese señor es **un autor español**.	*That gentleman is a Spanish author.*
Mi amigo Miguel conoce **al cónsul japonés**.	*My friend Mike knows the Japanese consul.*
Los Ángeles es una ciudad con **tráfico muy congestionado**.	*Los Angeles is a city with very congested traffic.*
Escribió **una novela muy fascinante**.	*He wrote a very fascinating novel.*
Sus **amigos** son **bastante ricos**.	*His friends are plenty rich.*

Next, there are many adjectives that seem to "go with" certain nouns; that is, they denote normal, expected characteristics of the nouns: it is normal and expected for snow to be white, blood is always red, and so on. Such adjectives are commonly placed before the nouns they modify, just as in English.

La roja sangre de los patriotas, derramada por la libertad.	*The red blood of patriots, spilled for liberty.*
Los osos polares pasaron silenciosamente por **la blanca nieve**.	*The polar bears went silently across the white snow.*

Whenever a descriptive and a quantitative adjective modify one noun, the word order is as follows:

article or possessive or demonstrative adjective +
quantitative adjective + noun + descriptive adjective

Notice that cardinal numbers have no gender.

¿**Las cinco rosas rojas** del jardín? Se las di a mi hija.	*The five red roses from the garden? I gave them to my daughter.*
Llamé a **mis cuatro primas bonitas**.	*I called my four pretty cousins. (This also indicates the subject has cousins who are not pretty! English speakers would stress the word pretty to indicate this.)*
Llamé a **mis cuatro bonitas primas**.	*I called my four pretty cousins. (This does not imply the existence of ugly cousins!)*
Tengo **estos cuatro discos compactos** en mi colección.	*I have these four CDs in my collection.*

Finally, there are several high-frequency descriptive adjectives in Spanish whose placement with respect to the noun makes their meaning change. In the examples that follow the complete list here, notice that when these adjectives are placed in the normal, post-nominal position, their meaning is literal, but when they are placed before the noun (pre-nominal), their meaning is figurative. One way to remember this is to think of their special, pre-nominal placement as making their meaning special.

Note that the forms **grande** and **alguno** (just as the ordinal numbers **primero** and **tercero**) shorten before singular masculine nouns to **gran**, and **algún** (**primer** and **tercer**).

ADJECTIVE	POST-NOMINAL (LITERAL)	PRE-NOMINAL (FIGURATIVE)
antiguo	*ancient*	*former*
alguno/algún	*any at all*	*some*
bajo	*short*	*low, as in vile*
caro	*expensive*	*beloved*
cierto	*definite, certain*	*a certain*
dichoso	*lucky, blessed*	*annoying, despicable*
grande/gran	*large*	*important, great*
medio	*average*	*half*
mismo/a	*himself/herself*	*same, (the very)*
nuevo	*brand new*	*another*
pobre	*poor (no money)*	*unlucky, unfortunate*
propio	*proper, suitable*	*own*
raro	*strange, odd, weird*	*rare (few)*
único	*unique*	*only*
viejo	*elderly*	*old (from long ago)*

Mi antiguo profesor de filosofía me inspiró con su amor a las letras.

My former philosophy professor inspired me with his love of literature.

Tengo **un escritorio antiguo** que uso para estudiar.

I have an old desk that I use for studying.

Juan tiene **un nuevo carro** que compró de su amigo.

John has a new car that he bought from his friend. (used, just another car)

Yo prefiero comprar **un carro nuevo**, no de segunda mano.

I prefer to buy a brand-new car, not a second-hand one.

La pobre profesora no ha podido publicar ni una línea.

The unfortunate professor has not been able to publish so much as one line.

Esos hombres pobres siempre van a la iglesia para comer.

Those poor men (men who don't have any money) always go to the church to eat.

Tengo **mi propio laptop** y no lo comparto con nadie.

I have my own laptop and I don't share it with anyone.

El uso propio de una laptop es escribir y buscar información en la red.

The proper use of a laptop is for writing and looking for information on the web.

A ver si no encuentro **algún lápiz** con qué escribir el número de teléfono.

Let's see if I can't find some pencil to write down the phone number.

Mira como no hay **lápiz alguno** por aquí.

Well look at that; there's not any pencil around here at all.

Translate the following short noun clauses into Spanish.

1. the third building _____

2. the poor boy (i.e., unfortunate) _____

3. the first five winners _____

4. the first car _____

5. a half an hour _____

6. the tall French woman _____

7. the only cat _____

8. the big dogs _____

9. the last book _____

10. my own backpack _____

11. the yellow sun _____

12. my old girlfriend (i.e., former) _____

13. the nine red apples _____

14. some poor children (i.e., no money) _____

15. some very beautiful houses _____

16. a fascinating story _____

17. some long nights _____

18. a weird old man _____

19. the great hero _____

20. the first girl _____

*Select the Spanish translation that is both grammatically correct and that properly
and best translates the following English sentences.*

1. Alexandra is a very diligent student.

   a. Alexandra es una muy aplicada alumna.

   b. Alexandra es una alumna muy aplicada.

   c. Alexandra es muy diligente como aplicada.

2. I saw Mr. Gómez's *tall* daughter yesterday.

   a. Vi ayer a la alta hija del Sr. Gómez.

   b. Ayer, vi a la hija alta del Sr. Gómez.

   c. El Sr. Gómez tiene una hija alta y la vi ayer.

3. There were several little girls playing jump rope in the garden
   this morning.

   a. Jugaban en el jardín esta mañana varias muchachas que saltaban la soga.

   b. Había varias niñitas que jugaban a saltar la soga en el jardín esta mañana.

   c. En el jardín esta mañana, había muchas niñas que jugaban a saltar la soga.

4. I met three Russian businessmen last night.

   a. Conocí a tres empresarios rusos anoche.

   b. Tres rusos, comerciantes todos, me conocieron anoche.

   c. Anoche encontré a tres empresarios de Rusia.

5. Isn't there a single book here worth reading?

   a. ¿Hay algún libro aquí que valga la pena leer?

   b. ¿No hay libro alguno aquí que valga la pena leer?

   c. ¿No hay buenos libros aquí que quisiera leer?

6. John has an old fountain pen worth $500.

   a. La pluma fuente antigua que tiene Juan vale $500.

   b. Juan tiene una pluma fuente antigua que vale $500.

   c. La antigua pluma fuente de Juan vale $500.

7. Is there some backpack for the trip to Mount Rainier?

   a. ¿Habrá una mochila para el viaje a la montaña de Rainier?

   b. ¿Hay alguna mochila para el viaje a la montaña de Rainier?

   c. A ver si no hay una mochila para el viaje a la montaña de Rainier.

8. Alexandra has her very own laptop for doing homework.

   a. La misma laptop que tiene Alexandra es para hacer la tarea.

   b. Alexandra tiene su propia laptop para hacer la tarea.

   c. La propia laptop de Alexandra es para hacer la tarea.

9. They just bought a new house (from a previous owner).

   a. Ellos ya compraron una casa nueva.

   b. Ellos acaban de comprar una nueva casa.

   c. Ellos acaban de comprar una casa nueva.

10. They have their own car so they don't need to rent one.

    a. Ya que tienen su propio carro, no tienen que alquilar uno.

    b. Tienen su propio carro, de modo que no necesitan alquilar uno.

    c. Ellos tienen un carro propio, de modo que no tienen que alquilar uno.

11. She read that very novel last night!

    a. ¡Ella misma leyó esa novela anoche!

    b. ¡Ella leyó esa misma novela anoche!

    c. ¡Anoche mismo ella leyó la novela!

12. There was a certain house with a bad reputation in that neighborhood.

    a. Había cierta casa de mala fama en ese barrio.

    b. Había una casa cierta de mala fama en ese barrio.

    c. Había en ese barrio una cierta casa de mala fama.

13. She and Michelle haven't published a single article in several years.

    a. Hace años que ni ella ni Michelle publican nada.

    b. Ella y Michelle no han publicado artículo alguno en varios años.

    c. Ella y Michelle no tienen ningún artículo publicado en varios años.

14. The proper use of the hammer is to pound nails.

    a. El propio martillo es para poner clavos.

    b. El uso propio del martillo es poner clavos.

    c. El propio uso del martillo es poner clavos.

15. Her former husband was a crook.

    a. Su esposo antiguo fue criminal.

    b. Fue criminal el ex-esposo de ella.

    c. Su antiguo esposo era criminal.

Demonstrative adjectives, demonstrative pronouns, and neuter pronouns

Demonstrative adjectives

Demonstrative adjectives point to a word in a more focused way than articles in that they anchor them in space and even in time. Consider how they do this in English. To say *this car* as opposed to *the car* or *a car* seems to bestow coordinates on the car, a sort of verbal GPS! Demonstrative adjectives show this same focusing characteristic when we say, for instance, *that day* or *those days* as opposed to *the day* or *the days*, or even less specifically *a day* or *someday* or *a few days*. Thus, demonstrative adjectives also have been compared to verbal index fingers that point at an object in space or to an event in time.

In English, we have only four demonstrative adjectives: *this* and its plural, *these*; *that* and its plural *those*. Note that the difference between them is to show relative distance from the speaker (in space or time) along with singular and plural forms. There are two "distances" in English. Spanish has three sets of demonstratives, one of which denotes a psychologically more remote distance in space or time. In addition, the fact that Spanish has gender and number, makes a total of twelve demonstrative adjectives. The following list shows these forms, beginning with the nearest of the three distances. There is no adequate translation into English for the last set unless you mentally tack on phrases such as *over yonder* or *way over there*.

	THIS	THESE	THAT	THOSE	THAT (FURTHER)	THOSE (FURTHER)
MASCULINE	este	estos	ese	esos	aquel	aquellos
FEMININE	esta	estas	esa	esas	aquella	aquellas

Besides the requirement that these adjectives must agree in gender and number with the nouns they modify (just as articles must), there are five things to keep in mind when using them:

- In Spanish as in English, you can only use either one article or one demonstrative or possessive adjective (such as *my* or *your*) before a noun, never two.
- No other word can ever come between a demonstrative adjective and the noun it points to.
- The singular masculine forms do not end in a final -**o**, but their plurals conform to that gender marker.
- Do not mistakenly use the neuter pronouns **esto** and **eso** as if they were demonstrative adjectives (these are also treated in this chapter).

31

- Do not confuse the feminine singular **esta** or the feminine plural **estas** with **está** and **estás**, which are forms of the verb **estar**. The accent on the final -a in the verb shows the stress to be on the last syllable. The demonstrative adjectives do not have that accent and are always, therefore, stressed on the first syllable: **e-.**

Examine these contrastive examples to see how the demonstrative adjectives work in this short dialogue. The first two lines are said by one person and the third is a question from a second person, at that second person's house. In other words, the first speaker is visiting and is wearing the shirt spoken of in the first line. The pants are in a shopping bag on a sofa a few feet away:

—Compré **esta camisa** en un mercado al aire libre en Quezaltenango.	*I bought this shirt in an open-air market in Quezaltenango.*
—Pero **esos pantalones**, los compré aquí, en Estados Unidos.	*But those pants, I bought them here, in the United States.*
—Ah, ya veo. Pero, **aquel sombrero** que vi en tu casa, ¿dónde lo compraste?	*Oh, I see. But, where did you buy that hat I saw at your house?*

Demonstrative pronouns

The forms of the demonstrative pronouns are exactly the same as the demonstrative adjectives except that in writing they bear an orthographical accent. As pronouns, they stand in for a noun that is understood and has been absorbed, as it were, into the adjective form. This is known as *substantivization* of an adjective, that is, turning an adjective into, in this case, a pronoun that in turn stands for a noun. This is done in English all the time when, for example, in response to a question such as "Do you like this shirt or that shirt?" we might answer simply "That one" or even just "That." So this aspect of the usage of the demonstrative adjectives should be easy; they simply convert into pronouns by omitting the noun that they obviously refer to. First, however, let's examine the forms; after that, we'll take a look at how this process occurs. Remember, these words are pronounced exactly like the demonstrative adjectives they come from:

	THIS ONE	THESE	THAT ONE	THOSE	THAT ONE (FURTHER)	THOSE (FURTHER)
MASCULINE	éste	éstos	ése	ésos	aquél	aquéllos
FEMININE	ésta	éstas	ésa	ésas	aquélla	aquéllas

Although the Spanish Royal Academy officially eliminated the requirement for using the accents on demonstrative pronouns, adherence to their edicts is far from uniform. Many conservative presses continue to use them and, of course, they will be found in any books printed prior to the official change. So don't be surprised if you see them with or without accents, since any book printed prior to the changes will still have them.

Imagine you're in a store, shopping for a shirt. On shelves that go along a wall and up to the ceiling are many colors of one particular style. You start comparing the colors of shirts. Pay attention to what happens to the demonstrative adjectives. They're easy to identify because they are always followed by a noun. The demonstrative pronouns will not have a noun after them—they've absorbed them!

Creo que me gusta más **esta camisa verde**.	*I think I like this green shirt best.*
Pero, todavía es muy atractiva **ésa de color café**.	*But that coffee-colored one is still quite attractive.*
A ver, ¿entonces **aquélla, la de color de naranja** no te agrada?	*Let's see, so, you don't like that one, the orange-colored one up there?*

The fact that there are gender markers as well as singular and plural—and three distances—makes both demonstrative adjectives and pronouns very useful, economical, and powerful little words. They enable speakers to keep things straight.

Neuter pronouns

There are a handful of neuter pronouns in Spanish. You may wonder why Spanish would need such a thing, since either the masculine or feminine genders are attached to every noun in the language. They exist because often we speak of more abstract things to which no noun is attached, for instance, a body of information such as is contained in a speech or article. In English, we often address these phenomena using verbal formulae such as "all that which was said" or colloquially, "all that" or even "all that stuff." Spanish has five neuter pronouns, shown as follows. The most common English translations are shown as well. Among these five forms, **ello** is found in somewhat formal writing (and even formal speech); despite occasional protestations that its use is rare, I frequently find it in newspapers from both sides of the Atlantic, so it is worth recognizing.

aquello	*that*
ello	*it*
eso	*that*
esto	*this*
lo	*it*

Most uses of neuter pronouns have to do with references to speech acts either in the present or the past. So the same observations about distance in space or time apply with regard to the forms that resemble the demonstrative adjectives and pronouns: **esto**, (something in the immediate present), **eso** (something in the immediate past or even in the present), and **aquello** (something more remote in the past that requires some recollection).

Pues, no entiendo **esto**.	*Well, I don't understand this.*
¿Escuchaste **eso**?	*Did you hear that?*
No entendí **aquello** que explicaba el profe la semana pasada.	*I didn't understand that stuff the prof was explaining last week.*
Los portavoces de la administración se negaron a elaborar sobre **ello**.	*Administrative spokespersons refused to elaborate about it.*

Using lo

The neuter pronoun **lo** is quite interesting, useful, and important. As you know, there is no subject pronoun in Spanish that corresponds to the English word *it* when *it* is used as a subject pronoun. In other words, to say *It is snowing*, you simply say **Está nevando** or even just **Nieva**. Likewise, *It is interesting* is simply **Es interesante**.

However, the word **lo**, placed before an adjective, creates an abstract, singular subject in the third-person, but only in combination with the adjective. This little device makes it possible to start a sentence by saying, for instance, **Lo interesante**, which means *The interesting thing*. Often, an adverb is inserted between **lo** and the adjective to intensify it.

Lo **más triste** de todo eso es que perdió su billetera.	The saddest part in all that is that he lost his wallet.
Lo **menos divertido** fue el viaje por el desierto.	The least fun part was the trip through the desert.
Lo **mejor** es que mi esposa podrá acompañarme.	The best thing is that my wife will be able to come with me.

5·1

Translate the following short phrases into Spanish.

1. these two (female) students _____

2. this hat _____

3. this first mountain _____

4. those paintings _____

5. that light (in the distance) _____

6. this museum _____

7. those old books _____

8. this antique mirror _____

9. that box of books (way over there) _____

10. this friendly dog _____

11. this red shirt _____

12. that thin woman _____

13. that class _____

14. these pretty dresses _____

15. these brown shoes _____

16. those soccer players _____

17. that man over there _____

18. that sailboat yonder _____

19. these six brand new cars _____

20. this old house _____

Select the Spanish translation that is both grammatically correct and best reflects the meaning of the following English sentences.

1. These are the books Dr. Ramírez was talking to us about last night.

   a. Éstos son los libros de los cuales nos hablaba el Dr. Ramírez anoche.

   b. Esos libros son los de que el Dr. Ramírez nos habló anoche.

   c. El Dr. Ramírez nos habló de aquellos libros anoche.

2. I didn't understand any of that.

   a. No entiendo esto para nada.

   b. Yo no entendí nada de eso.

   c. Nada entiendo de aquello.

3. That despicable guy burns me up.

   a. Ese hombre me cae mal.

   b. El tipo ese me cae gordo.

   c. Aquel hombre me da asco.

4. I don't even want to lay eyes on that woman.

   a. Ni siquiera deseo verla.

   b. A la mujer esa no la quiero ver ni en pintura.

   c. No quiero ver a esa mujer más.

5. Didn't you see that movie with your girlfriend?

   a. ¿Fuiste al cine con tu novia para ver esa película?

   b. ¿No viste esa película con tu novia?

   c. ¿No fueron tú y tu novia a ver esa película?

6. Those were different times.

   a. Esos tiempos eran diferentes.

   b. Aquélla fue otra época.

   c. Esos fueron tiempos diferentes.

7. This guy is a great friend of mine.

    a. Este señor es mi buen amigo.

    b. Éste es gran amigo mío.

    c. Éste es mi amigo grande.

8. For *that*, it's important to research the subject in detail.

    a. Para ello, es importante investigar la materia a fondo.

    b. Para realizarlo, es importante investigar la materia a fondo.

    c. Por eso, es importante investigar la materia a fondo.

9. The professor's presentation was the best part of the conference.

    a. La presentación del profesor fue la mejor parte de la conferencia.

    b. La presentación del profesor es la parte que más me gustó de la conferencia.

    c. La presentación del profesor fue lo mejor de la conferencia.

10. The most fun part was when that woman tried to dance the tango.

    a. Lo más divertido fue cuando esa mujer quiso bailar el tango.

    b. La parte más divertida fue cuando esa mujer trató de bailar el tango.

    c. El momento más divertido fue cuando la mujer esa intentó bailar el tango.

11. Well, I don't know. This is a mystery.

    a. Bueno, no sé. Es misterioso.

    b. Pues, no sé. Esto es un misterio.

    c. Esto, pues, no lo sé; es misterioso.

12. Don't say anything about what happened yesterday.

    a. No digas nada sobre ayer.

    b. No hables nada sobre lo que pasó ayer.

    c. No digas nada sobre lo de ayer.

13. I told the whole thing to the lawyer, which seemed to him a scandalous matter.

    a. Se lo conté todo al abogado y le pareció un escándalo.

    b. Le conté todo al abogado, lo cual le pareció un asunto escandaloso.

    c. Le dije todo al abogado y eso le pareció escandaloso.

14. Here's the one (woman) I told you about that night a while back.

    a. Aquí está ésa de quien te hablé aquella noche.

    b. Aquí, es la mujer de quien te hablé esa noche.

    c. Allí está esa mujer de quien te hablé aquella noche.

15. Let's see the guest list . . . is this woman here?

    a. A ver la lista de los invitados ... ¿Está ésta?

    b. Pásame la lista de los invitados ... ¿Es ésta?

    c. Veamos la lista ... ¿Dónde está ésta?

Reflexive pronouns

One of the first conjugations that often challenges students is the infinitive form of reflexive verbs that have -**se** tacked onto them, for example, **lavarse**. For most students, it is not the concept of reflexivity that causes their difficulty. Rather, they do not realize that in the infinitive form the -**se** of the reflexive infinitive means *oneself*. When conjugated, this pronoun takes on the person and number of the subject. It helps to dissect this form to see just how simple it really is.

lavar + se	lavarse	*to wash oneself*
llamar + se	llamarse	*to call oneself*
vestir + se	vestirse	*to dress oneself*
poner + se	ponerse	*to put (something) on oneself*
quitar + se	quitarse	*to take (something) off of oneself*

Notice that each of these verbs can be used without the reflexive pronoun, but then that action performed by the subject will not be performed on the subject but on someone or something else. The verb will no longer be reflexive, as in the following examples:

Juan **lava** el carro.	*John washes the car.*
Mi amigo **me llamó** anoche.	*My friend called me last night.*
La mamá **le quitó** el juguete al niñito.	*The mom took the toy away from the little boy.*

When a verb is used reflexively, the various forms of the reflexive pronouns must be used, and those as well as the verb must agree in person and number with the subject. Here we will examine the verb **llamarse** conjugated in the present indicative and then in the preterit to demonstrate that regardless of tense, these same pronouns must be used if the verb is to be reflexive:

PRESENT INDICATIVE		PRETERITE	
me lavo	nos lavamos	me lavé	nos lavamos
te lavas	os laváis	te lavaste	os lavasteis
se lava	se lavan	se lavó	se lavaron

The process of changing the forms of the reflexive pronouns is called *declension* rather than *conjugation*, but the idea and process are similar. The reflexive pronoun, attached to the infinitive ending, is moved to a position in front of the verb, which is then conjugated. Note that the third-person singular and plural is **se** and that since the third person includes **él, ella,** and **usted** in the singular and **ellos, ellas,** and **ustedes** in the plural, this pronoun could refer to six objects: three in the singular and three in the plural. In its role as a reflexive object pronoun, **se** can mean the following things:

- **se** = *himself, herself, yourself* (when the speaker uses the formal **usted** form of address)
- **se** = *themselves* (masculine, feminine, or mixed group) and *yourselves* (using **ustedes** as the formal form of address or in Latin America for both formal and informal address)

The person and number of the pronoun changes in tandem with the person and number endings of the verb. If the verb is negative, the word **no** comes before the pronoun. As will be seen in subsequent chapters dealing with the various forms of object pronouns, nothing can ever be placed between the object pronoun or pronouns of any type and the verb.

Juan no **se lavó** las manos.	*John didn't wash his hands.*

In Chapter 1 on articles, we saw that the definite article is used with parts of the body and clothing, instead of the possessive adjectives. Now you can see the reason why more clearly. Reflexive pronouns obviate any need for the redundancy of using the possessive—unless there is a need to point out that the ownership of, say, an article of clothing used by the subject does not belong to the subject. In the first example here, you can see that the default interpretation about the ownership falls to the use of the reflexive pronoun, and so the ownership is assumed to correspond to the subject who is also the object. In the second example, you can see how that usual assumption is corrected when the ownership of the article of clothing (in this instance) does not correspond to, or follow, that of the object pronoun. The action is still reflexive, however, because Juana dresses herself in both cases.

Juana **se puso** la falda para ir a la fiesta.	*Jane put on her skirt in order to go to the party.*
Juana **se puso** la falda de su hermana para ir a la fiesta.	*Jane put on her sister's skirt in order to go to the party.*

Before summarizing the uses of **se**, remember that all reflexive pronouns are often used simply to make an action or a command emphatic. Here are two commonly heard examples:

Juan **se fue**.	*John took off (left in haste).*
¡**Tómate** las vitaminas!	*Drink up (take) your vitamins!*

The uses of se

The use of **se** is frequently presented in standard textbooks either with or before direct object pronouns. More importantly, **se** is almost always presented before students learn about indirect object pronouns. There is nothing wrong with this; much of the confusion about object pronouns is unavoidable. The human, real-time learning curve to absorb what is presented and be able to use it properly is longer than the academic calendar.

The pronoun **se** may refer to a third-person as a reflexive pronoun, as seen previously. It can appear as the form it must assume when **le** or **les** would otherwise precede the direct, third-person object pronouns **lo, la, los,** or **las**. This is one of the difficulties of what is usually labeled *double object pronouns*, when both an indirect and a direct object pronoun are used in a sentence. Note that the indirect always appears first. Any of the indirect object pronouns in the table here may be followed by any of the direct object pronouns in the right-hand column.

INDIRECT	DIRECT
me	lo
te	la
nos	los
os	las
se	

Just as it did as a reflexive object pronoun, **se** may refer to six grammatical persons as indirect objects: **a él, a ella,** and **a ustedes** when **se** is derived from **le,** and **a ellos, a ellas,** and **a ustedes** when **se** is derived from **les.** One way to accept that this arrangement is reasonable is to recognize that reflexive objects are simply a special case of indirect objects in which the receiver of the action also happens to be the subject of the verb.

The pronoun **se** may also function to form what is known as the pseudo-passive construction that can only translate into English either as a passive construction or, more colloquially, as employing some use of *get* or *got.* When translated literally, this third-person construction makes it appear as if things did something to themselves. This of course is silly (see parentheses in the examples below), but it can actually help some learners recognize this structure when they hear or see it and thus absorb and use it correctly.

Se rompió la ventana.	*The window was broken.*
	The window got broken.
	(The window broke itself.)
Se abrieron las ventanas.	*The windows were opened.*
	The windows opened up.
	(The windows opened themselves.)

There is another way in which this structure is used. You may have encountered it in your textbook as a way to express unexpected occurrences or as a way to show that a person is affected by an action. Here's how it works: The indirect object pronoun of the person affected is placed between **se** and the verb. In the following example, a literal translation of **se ... perdió** makes it appear that the glove lost itself. The presence of **me** in between shows that I am the person affected by the loss (and furthermore, deflects any responsibility or carelessness on my part!). If the third-person pronoun is used to show the person affected, then a clarifier is frequently needed, as shown in the second example. Note that **se ... descompuso** still makes it appear that the car broke itself and **le,** clarified in the second example by **A Juan,** tells us who owns the car and who was impacted by the event. The third example shows how this construction works by presenting one instance in which everything is plural. The fourth example has a parallel in colloquial English, shown by the second translation.

Se me perdió un guante.	*My glove got lost.*
A Juan **se le descompuso** el carro.	*John's car broke down.*
A Tere y Marta **se les quemaron** los pasteles.	*Tere's and Marta's cakes got burned.*
Al granjero **se le murió** la vaca.	*The farmer's cow died.*
	The farmer's cow up and died on him.

The pronoun **se** also forms what is known as the impersonal **se** construction, corresponding roughly to *one does this or that* or to what is sometimes called the "editorial or impersonal you" in English. It is common in ads and other forms of signage. The one most familiar to English speakers is the first example. The last one, which I picked up from a bulletin board in a northern Virginia shooting range, is from a real wanted poster issued by Colombia in the mid 1990s for the notorious leader of the Medellín drug cartel.

Se habla español aquí.	*Spanish spoken here.*
Se vende carro.	*Car for sale.*
Se alquila.	*For rent.*
Se busca. Emilio Escobar.	*Wanted: Emilio Escobar.*

Finally, when it comes to the Spanish pronoun system, the third person is where nearly all the troubles lie. There can be, as noted with **se,** six possible persons (three singular and three plural) to whom a third-person pronoun might refer. Let's ignore the other persons and numbers for a moment and isolate the forms of all pronouns in the third person.

The first difficulty was addressed in the chapter about forms of address: the fact that **usted** and **ustedes** are second person in meaning but take the third-person verb forms. Their corresponding object pronouns follow the third person.

Subject Pronouns

SINGULAR	PLURAL
él	ellos
ella	ellas
usted	ustedes

Reflexive Object Pronouns

SINGULAR	PLURAL
se	se

Indirect Object Pronouns

SINGULAR	PLURAL
le	les

Le and **les** become **se** before **lo**, **la**, **los**, and **las**, as was summarized and explained previously when dealing with double object pronouns.

Juan **se lo** dio a María.	*John gave **it to Mary**.*
Se lo dijimos ayer.	*We said **it to them** yesterday.*

Direct Object Pronouns

SINGULAR	PLURAL
lo	los
la	las

Direct object pronouns replace previously mentioned nouns and, when in the third person, show the gender and number of the nouns. Observe in the following examples how the direct object nouns are replaced by direct object pronouns.

Compré dos manzanas.	**Las** compré.	*I bought them.*
Vendió los carros.	**Los** vendió.	*He/She/You sold them.*

Observe how an indirect object is added to show someone receiving the direct objects:

Juan **me** dio las manzanas.	*John gave me the apples. (indirect object pronoun, but direct object noun)*
Juan **me las** dio.	*John gave them to me. (both objects expressed as pronouns)*
Juan **le** dio las manzanas (a Marta).*	*John gave the apples to Marta.*
Juan **se las** dio (a Marta).*	*John gave them to her.*

---

*a Marta would only be used to avoid confusion.

When the third-person finds itself an object of a preposition, the subject form is used, except when reflexive, as in the second example. The first- and second-person singular forms are more problematic, ironically.

In the first- and second-person singular, the forms of the object of a preposition are **mí** and **ti** (note the orthographical accent in **mí**, to distinguish it from the possessive adjective **mi**). When the preposition **con** is used, these become **conmigo** and **contigo**, respectively, as shown by the last two examples.

Juan fue **con ella**.	*John went with her.*
María se lo llevó **consigo** misma.	*Mary took it with her (herself).*
¿Quieres ir **conmigo** al cine?	*Do you want to go to the movies with me?*
¡Por supuesto! Siempre me gusta ir **contigo**.	*Of course! I always like going with you.*

EJERCICIO
6·1

Identify the English translations on the right that match the Spanish sentences on the left. Focusing on the pronoun usage as well as the verbs will help you sort them out.

_____ 1. Se lo dio a su papá.

_____ 2. Se necesita valor para ir allá.

_____ 3. Después de vestirse, se fue.

_____ 4. Se busca. Gato perdido.

_____ 5. Se cayó la lámpara.

_____ 6. El carro se resbaló.

_____ 7. La casa se incendió.

_____ 8. Ella se enamoró de él.

_____ 9. La billetera se le perdió.

_____ 10. Se lo otorgaron.

_____ 11. Ellos se enamoraron.

_____ 12. Para aprender, se tiene que estudiar.

_____ 13. Se me ocurrió una idea fantástica.

_____ 14. Los viejos se mueren de viejos.

_____ 15. Se pintaron las casas de azul.

_____ 16. Se besaron tras la ceremonia.

_____ 17. Él se caerá en su propia trampa.

a. He will fall into his own trap.

b. The house burned down.

c. They awarded it to her.

d. They fell in love.

e. He'll be charged as a criminal.

f. His dad gave it to my cousin.

g. A great idea came to me.

h. They kissed after the ceremony.

i. The lamp fell down.

j. Old people die of old age.

k. The houses were painted blue.

l. The car skidded.

m. The meeting slipped our mind.

n. He lost his wallet.

o. Lost cat.

p. To learn, you have to study.

q. He gave it to his dad.

_____ 18. Se le acusará de ser criminal.

_____ 19. Su papá se lo regaló a mi primo.

_____ 20. Se nos pasó la cita por completo.

r.   She fell in love with him.

s.   You need courage to go there.

t.   After getting dressed, he left.

EJERCICIO
6·2

Translate the following sentences from Spanish to English.

1. ¿Sabe Ud. si se alquila un piso en este edificio?

_____

2. Juan y María se fueron corriendo cuando oyeron el estallido de la bomba.

_____

3. Por varias horas después del incidente, no se oía nada.

_____

4. ¿La tarea? Se la comió el perro.

_____

5. Ay, ¡tómate la medicina y ya!

_____

6. Este anillo antiguo me lo regaló un amigo.

_____

7. El Sr. Martínez se levantó, tomó la propuesta de la mesa y se la llevó consigo mismo.

_____

8. ¿Se lo dijiste a ellos? Pero, hombre—¡Era un secreto!

_____

9. Se nos descompuso el auto en la carretera y tuvimos que llamar a mi tío.

_____

10. ¿La postal? Se la mandé ayer a nuestros papás.

_____

11. ¿Cómo se prepara una buena ensalada, mamá?

_____

12. Un regalo para ti. Fui con mi hermano para comprártelo.

_____

13. El jefe necesita el martillo, présteselo, pues.

_____

14. El mecánico tiene las manos sucias. Se las va a lavar antes de usar el teléfono.

_____

15. ¿Qué hago yo día tras día? Pues, nada menos que lo que se tiene que hacer.

_____

16. ¿La factura para Don Tomás? Estoy preparándosela ahorita.

_____

17. ¿Quieres ver esa película conmigo o con él?

_____

18. Los novios se miraban todo el tiempo.

_____

19. Ese tipo parece loco—todo el tiempo se habla a sí mismo.

_____

20. El Sr. Acero no se avergüenza ni cuando se revelan sus mentiras.

_____

Translate the following sentences from English to Spanish.

1. How do you make a good salad?

_____

2. The baby fell down.

_____

3. The plate got broken.

_____

4. She put on a new pair of shoes.

_____

5. The dog licked his paws.

_____

6. He got well quickly.

_____

7. They went straight up the mountain!

_____

8. The sweater came apart before she could finish knitting it.

_____

9. They promised to love each other.

_____

10. We were looking for each other all day.

_____

11. We gave them (plates) to her.

_____

12. They became teachers.

_____

13. She combed her hair and put on makeup.

_____

14. I sold it (painting) to them.

_____

15. The shirt was hung on a hanger.

_____

16. She was glad you had called her.

_____

17. In Macondo, the houses were not painted red.

_____

18. He was surprised by the noise.

_____

19. This letter was written in the nineteenth century.

_____

20. The stockings were hung by the chimney with care.

_____

Use all the elements in each series of words to create grammatically correct sentences in Spanish. You'll have to add some details such as articles and prepositions. Note that only the dictionary forms of nouns, verbs, and adjectives are supplied, so be careful with agreement rules and pay attention to clues for the tense of the verbs.

1. Él/mirarse/espejo/ayer.

_____

2. Ellos/comprarse/regalos/anoche.

_____

3. Zapatos/perderse/esta mañana/playa.

_____

4. Anoche/vino/derramarse/mesa.

_____

5. Ese día/campanas/repicarse/celebrar la paz.

_____

6. Sr. Acero/condenarse/pronto.

_____

7. Ellas/creerse/lo máximo.

_____

8. Niños/dormirse/las ocho/ayer.

_____

9. Ella/levantarse/las siete/mañana.

_____

10. Ellos/enojarse/tú/no hacer/tarea/ayer.

_____

11. Bebé/tomarse/leche/ahora.

_____

12. Juan y María/abrazarse/anoche/parque.

_____

13. Mientras/ella/vestirse/anoche/ellos/dormirse/sofá.

_____

14. Anoche/yo/escribir/carta/ellos. (*Use object pronouns. Make a four word sentence*)

_____

15. Juan/enojarse/irse.

_____

16. Hansel/no perderse/bosque/nunca.

_____

17. Mantequilla/derretirse/si/no ponerse/nevera.

_____

18. Perderse/juicio/Don Quijote.

_____

19. Cómo/escribirse/su nombre?

_____

20. Él/ir a esquiar/ayer/rompérsele/pierna.

_____

Double object pronouns

If you are like most students, you were probably exposed to indirect object pronouns without their being identified as such. In an early chapter of most textbooks, students are often taught a few phrases involving the verb **gustar** to provide them with some groundwork for using Spanish in class. When most texts introduce object pronouns in a deliberate manner, they start with the direct object pronouns. This is fine, but, since students learn the direct object pronouns first, they may become confused later when they have to learn to use both types in one verb phrase. As a result, they often put the direct object first.

Besides that, at a more cognitive level, there are two other obstacles. First, students tend not to perceive the different functions of these two classes of object pronouns. Secondly, the forms of all but the third-person indirect and direct pronouns are identical. The object pronoun **me**, for instance, can be either direct or indirect:

Marta **me** vio.	*Marta saw **me**. (**me** is a direct object pronoun)*
Marta **me** dio una galleta.	*Marta gave **me** a cookie. (**me** is an indirect object)*

As was seen in Chapter 6, object pronouns, especially direct object pronouns, are used when the noun they refer to has already been mentioned and need not be repeated—just as English uses *it* or *them*. Direct objects are the people, things, or even ideas that are acted upon directly. The question to ask in order to identify a direct object is "what?" As shown by the following example, using a noun as the direct object, the question to identify the direct object would be "What did I buy?"

Compré una rosa.	*I bought a rose.*

Thus, *what* did the subject (**yo**) buy? **Una rosa**. Therefore **una rosa** is the direct object of the verb **comprar** (*to buy*). Next, let's change the direct object noun into a direct object pronoun and observe what happens. Note first of all that the listener would have to know what **la** refers to—it would have been previously mentioned, just as is true when English uses *it* as a direct object.

La compré.	*I bought it.*

As was also seen in Chapter 6, an indirect object shows *to whom* or *for whom* an action is performed, either to help or hurt them. Indirect object pronouns are generally not optional if there is a receiver mentioned. When the receiver is **le** or **les** and followed by a direct object pronoun, a clarifier is often used, such as **a él** or **a ustedes**, to make it clear to whom the indirect object is referring. Since no confusion can happen with the first and second-person indirect objects, they do not require any clarifiers—and when they are used, such as **a mí**, it is for emphasis. It is easy to identify an indirect object when you ask the question *to* or *for whom* was the action performed? For the following example, the question needed to identify the indirect object would be specifically formulated as *For whom did I buy a rose?* You can quickly see that the person *for whom* the subject (**yo**) bought a rose is the person spoken to, as revealed by the use of the indirect object pronoun **te**. Note that when **para** is used to indicate a receiver (i.e., the indirect object, noun, or pronoun), the indirect object pronoun is omitted.

Yo **te compré** una rosa.	*I bought you a rose.*
	I bought a rose for you.
Yo compré una rosa **para ti**.	*I bought a rose for you.*
	I bought you a rose.
Yo compré una rosa **para ella**.	*I bought her a rose.*
	I bought a rose for her.

The most condensed way to express the last example above, when all objects are contextually clear to the listener, is to say:

Se la compré.	*I bought it for her.*

As you shall see shortly, object pronouns often can be placed in either of two positions. However, when there is only one conjugated verb involved, the indirect object pronoun must always be placed before the direct object pronoun, followed by the verb. If the sentence is negative, the negating word **no** comes before the object pronouns. The second translation of the example below is not the best English, but is common enough to admit, and, since it puts the objects in the same order as Spanish, it can be a useful starting point for understanding this in Spanish.

Te la compré.	*I bought it for you.*
	I bought you it.

Before proceeding to summarize and exemplify all the placement rules in outline form, let's look at all the indirect and direct object pronouns. Once again, we shall observe one of the functions of the object pronoun **se**, touched upon in the previous chapter.

The indirect object pronouns are:

me	nos
te	os
le/se	les/se

The direct object pronouns are:

me	nos
te	os
lo, la	los, las

As was stated in the previous chapter, most of the morphological (form) confusion experienced by learners faced with the Spanish pronoun system seems to reside in the third-person forms. When learners are confused about the other forms (**me**, **te**, **nos**, and **os**), it inevitably has to do with understanding the differences in grammatical functions among indirect, reflexive, and direct objects. For users of this volume who may not be proceeding linearly through the chapters, but instead using it as a reference work, what was said in the previous chapter about the use of **se** bears repeating, beginning with the chart that shows the possible combinations of **se**, which *must* be used whenever **le** or **les** otherwise would precede **lo**, **la**, **los**, or **las**:

INDIRECT	DIRECT
me	lo
te	la
nos	los
os	las
se	

The pronoun **se** may refer to six persons when it, of necessity, replaces **le** or **les**, which are indirect object pronouns. This can be confusing if not viewed analytically. Spanish has a way of dealing with the ambiguity which, of course, exists even when **le** or **les** are used. The grammatical mechanism whereby this is achieved is known as a *clarifying clause*, which begins with the preposition **a** (*to*). The following examples will demonstrate and model the use of clarifiers, using only **le** or **les**, and showing how they refer to all three possible uses of each of these indirect object pronouns. The second translations in each example show the way in which the English preposition *to* is used to mark the indirect object, or recipient, as a clarifier of **le** and **les**, just as the preposition **a** does in Spanish. At the same time, however, notice that the first translation reflects the Spanish word order with regard to the use of double object pronouns, which we shall soon examine in more detail.

Clarifiers of le

Yo **le** di el libro **a Juan**.
I gave John the book.
I gave the book to John.

Yo **le** di el libro **a Juana**.
I gave Jane the book.
I gave the book to Jane.

Yo **le** di el libro **a usted**.
I gave you the book.
I gave the book to you.

Clarifiers of les

Ella **les** vendió un carro nuevo **a Tomás y María**.
She sold Tom and Mary a new car.
She sold a new car to Tom and Mary.

Ella **les** vendió un carro nuevo **a María y Marta**.
She sold Mary and Martha a new car.
She sold a new car to Mary and Martha.

Ella **les** vendió un carro nuevo **a ustedes**.
She sold you a new car.
She sold a new car to you.

Now that we have seen how **le** and **les** are clarified, we can examine what happens when the noun phrases **el libro** and **un carro nuevo**, functioning as direct objects, are changed to a direct object pronoun. In this case **lo** is the pronoun used since the nouns are third-person, singular, and masculine. By using **lo**, and retaining the clarifying clauses, we can produce a useful synopsis of the various meanings that **se** has as an indirect object pronoun when used with any of the remaining third-person direct object pronouns: **la**, **los**, and **las**. Notice how, when English uses both pronouns, there is no mechanism for further identifying the true third-person recipient—*him*, *her*, or *them*—by name.

When **se** is used before a third-person verb (singular or plural) and is not followed by **lo**, **la**, **los**, or **las**, the use of **se** is either: reflexive, pseudo-passive, or impersonal, as explained in the previous chapter. When **se** is followed by **lo**, **la**, **los** or **las**, its function is that of an indirect object pronoun, replacing **le** or **les**. In the following examples, only the masculine singular direct object **lo** (*it*) is used following **se**. The direct object noun that **lo** represents is indicated in parentheses.

Clarifiers of **se** when it must replace **le**

Yo **se** lo di **a Juan**.	*I gave him it (the book).*
	I gave it (the book) to him.
Yo **se** lo di **a Juana**.	*I gave her it (the book).*
	I gave it (the book) to her.
Yo **se** lo di **a usted**.	*I gave you it (the book).*
	I gave it (the book) to you.

Clarifiers of **se** when it must replace **les**

Ella **se** lo vendió **a Tomás y María**.	*She sold them it (a new car).*
	She sold it (a new car) to them.
Ella **se** lo vendió **a María y Marta**.	*She sold them it (a new car).*
	She sold it (a new car) to them.
Ella **se** lo vendió **a ustedes**.	*She sold you it (a new car).*
	She sold it (a new car) to you.

Now that we've seen all the permutations involving **se**, let's examine where object pronouns can be placed in modern Spanish. There are four scenarios, two of which have options and two of which do not:

- **Scenario One (no options):** When a single conjugated verb is used, any and all object pronouns must precede the verb. If the sentence is negative, the word **no** will appear before the object pronoun or pronouns.

Juan **me lo vendió** ayer.	*John sold it to me yesterday.*
El Sr. Acero **no me lo** dijo honestamente.	*Mr. Acero did not say it to me honestly.*

- **Scenario Two (two options):** When a verb phrase involving the auxiliary (helping) verb **estar** (or any other verb that can form progressives) and a gerund (**-ando** and **-iendo** endings) is used, pronouns may either precede the conjugated helping verb or be appended (added to the end) of the gerund, as the following examples show.

Juan **estaba vendiéndomelo** ayer.	*John was selling it to me yesterday.*
Juan **me lo estaba vendiendo** ayer.	

  When pronouns are added to the gerund, a written accent is placed on the vowel of the stressed syllable of the gerund, to preserve the stress on that syllable.

- **Scenario Three (two options):** When a verb phrase involving an auxiliary verb and an infinitive is used, pronouns may either precede the conjugated helping verb or be appended to the infinitive, as the following examples show.

Juan **quería vendérmelo** ayer.	*John wanted to sell it to me yesterday.*
Juan **me lo quería vender** ayer.	

  When pronouns are added to the gerund, a written accent is placed on the vowel of the stressed syllable of the infinitive, to preserve the stress on that syllable. Since these are infinitives, the stress would fall on **-ár**, **-ér**, or **-ír**.

- **Scenario Four (no options):** With regard to commands or imperative forms, pronouns must be appended to the end of affirmative commands and the accent mark placed on the stressed syllable.

¡Véndamelo!   *Sell it to me!*

When pronouns are appended to the end of any verb form, an accent mark must be placed on the syllable that is stressed before they are added in order to indicate the preservation of its original pronunciation. However, when the command is negative, the object or objects must be detached and precede the verb, following the word **no**.

¡No **me lo venda**!   *Don't sell it to me!*

Now that we have seen how pronouns must or can be placed with respect to verbs in modern Spanish, we can examine the placement of object pronouns as found in older literature, features which still find their way into modern, formal writing and oratory.

In older literature and still often in formal oratory, editorials, and in many proverbs, you'll find object pronouns appended to the end of verbs. The tenses in which this phenomenon takes place most often are the present, the preterit, the imperfect, and the simple future.

Dígolo en serio.	*I say it in all seriousness.*
Fuese corriendo.	*He took off running.*
Vióme, acobardóse y **huyóme**, rabo entre las piernas.	*He saw me, turned coward, and fled from me, tail between his legs.*
Érase una vez...	*Once upon a time . . .*
Dirételo de una vez...	*I'll tell it to you all at once . . .*

Leístas and Loístas

The Spanish-speaking world is divided into two camps: **leístas** and **loístas**. The **leístas** hail from Spain—not Andalucía or the southern regions, but roughly from the central plateau northward. The southern and southwestern regions of Spain are, historically, **loístas**. Since most of the *conquistadores* came from southern regions—many from Extremadura—Latin America is overwhelmingly **loísta**.

For those readers who have no idea what I am referring to, according to the Royal Academy of the Language, **lo** is the third-person, masculine singular, direct object pronoun, used for **it, him,** or **you** (provided that **it** and **you** are masculine). According to the same august body, **le** is the third-person, singular, indirect object pronoun for both masculine and feminine.

Naturally, not everyone has always listened to the Royal Academy, and of course, Spanish was well established as a modern language by the time it was organized in the 1720s. By that time, many speakers from the geographical areas mentioned were already using **le** as a direct object pronoun—though only for the masculine—and the usage remains so to this day. The plurals are likewise impacted, so that it is common to hear or read <u>**Les** vi el otro día</u> (*I saw them the other day*—referring not merely to people, but only to a group of men) instead of (as the Royal Academy advises) <u>**Los** vi el otro día.</u>

Le and **les** are never used by **leístas** to refer to a human female direct object or objects. Why? Because it never has been done; it is not a part of their linguistic habit. **Leístas**, therefore, adhere to the Royal Academy's dictates when it comes to female direct objects, e.g., <u>**La** vi el otro día</u> or <u>**Las** vi el otro día</u> (*I saw her the other day* and *I saw them*—a group of women—*the other day*). As for what form to use to refer to indirect object(s), **leístas** and **loístas** are of one mind—they must be expressed using **le** or **les** (which changes to **se** if followed by any of the direct object pronouns **lo, la, los,** or **las**).

Match the English sentences with the Spanish; the cues in parentheses will help identify what direct object nouns are meant by the direct object pronouns in Spanish.

_____ 1.	They gave it (dress) to her.	a.	¡Escríbesela!
_____ 2.	She sold them (horses) to him.	b.	Se la quería traer.
_____ 3.	You're giving them (photos) to them.	c.	Espera contárselas.
_____ 4.	She wants to bring it (food) for her.	d.	¿Cuándo vas a mandársela?
_____ 5.	They couldn't send it (book) to him.	e.	Se la compró.
_____ 6.	Write him (a letter)!	f.	¡No se las vendan!
_____ 7.	He ought to repair it (car) for her.	g.	Estás dándoselas.
_____ 8.	He wanted to bring it (magazine) to her.	h.	¿Necesita llevárselos?
_____ 9.	I wanted to give it (coat) to her.	i.	Ella se los vendió.
_____ 10.	Don't sell them (tables) to her!	j.	Se la quiere traer.
_____ 11.	He hopes to tell them it (news).	k.	No pudieron enviárselo.
_____ 12.	When will you send her it (bill)?	l.	Debería arreglárselo.
_____ 13.	Buy them (flowers) for her!	m.	Quería dárselo.
_____ 14.	Don't read it (newspaper) to them!	n.	¡Présteselo!
_____ 15.	She bought it (necktie) for him.	o.	¡No se los compres!
_____ 16.	Loan them (the car)!	p.	Se la abrirán.
_____ 17.	Don't buy them (pencils) for her!	q.	Se los pidió.
_____ 18.	Does she need to take her them (plates)?	r.	¡Cómpraselas!
_____ 19.	They will open it (door) for her.	s.	¡No se lo lea!
_____ 20.	He ordered them (toys) for her.	t.	Se lo dieron.

Translate the following sentences into Spanish, using object pronouns for all noun objects of verbs.

1. She's washing his hands.

_____

2. We want to buy her a watch.

_____

3. Bring me the soap! (**tú**)

_____

4. She was hoping to find him some shoes.

_____

5. Don't send me the box!

_____

6. He should record the news for her.

_____

7. They are giving me gifts.

_____

8. He gave us wine for Christmas.

_____

9. They sent you the information yesterday. (**Ud.**)

_____

10. He will send them their photo.

_____

11. We want to make a web page for you. (**Uds.**)

_____

12. She didn't want to knit him a sweater.

_____

13. They brought us the tomatoes.

_____

14. She prepared the meal for them.

_____

15. We want to buy you a hat. (**tú**)

_____

16. They are building them a house.

_____

17. Don't buy me the shirt! (**tú** command)

_____

18. I should give the painting to him.

_____

19. Do you want to send them a postcard? (**tú**)

_____

20. We will not send you a bill. (**Ud.**)

_____

EJERCICIO

7·3

Use all the elements in each string to create grammatically correct sentences in Spanish, using only object pronouns for all noun objects of verbs. You'll have to add some details in most cases (e.g., articles and prepositions). When the position rules allow for more than one solution, show them both. Then translate them into English! Note that only the dictionary forms of nouns, verbs, and adjectives are supplied, so be careful with agreement rules and pay attention to clues for the tense of the verbs.

1. tú/querer/mandar/(libros)/(a él)/ahora.

_____

2. yo/tener/comprar/(blusa)/(para ella)/anoche.

_____

3. Nosotros/ir/vender/(coche)/(a Ud.)/la semana pasada.

_____

4. Ellos/no deber/servir/(cerveza)/(a los menores de edad).

_____

5. Tú/estar/escribir/(cuento)/(para ella)/en este momento.

_____

6. ¡Arreglar/(computadora)/(para nosotros)! (**tú** command)

_____

7. Él/traer/(teléfono)/(a mí) ayer.

_____

8. Yo/ir/poner/(demanda)/(al Sr. Acero)/pronto.

_____

9. Ella/hacer/(maleta)/(para mí)/esta mañana.

_____

10. Uds./querer/dar/(regalos)/(a los niños)/el fin de semana pasado.

_____

11. Los niños/romper/(ventana)/(a mí)/el domingo pasado.

_____

12. Ella/ir/pedir/(favor)/(a ellos)/mañana.

_____

13. ¡No/mandar/(carta)/(a ella)! (**Uds**. command)

_____

14. Nosotros/no poder/enviar/(mensaje)/(a ti)/ahora.

_____

15. Ella/querer/dar/(beso)/(a él)/anoche.

_____

16. Tú/deber/mostrar/(colección)/(a nosotros)/ahora.

_____

17. ¡Dar/(dinero)/(ellos)! (**Ud**. command)

_____

18. Yo/querer/pedir/(libros)/(a Ud.).

_____

19. Ella/ir/enviar/(cajas)/(a él)/esta tarde.

_____

20. Él/querer/escribir/(carta)/(a ella)/la semana pasada.

_____

Prepositions and translating English phrasal verbs

Prepositions comprise a small group of tiny words that do a great deal of heavy lifting in both English and Spanish. To begin, it is important to know what prepositions are and what they do.

First of all, prepositions are *relater* words. They express the relationship between two nouns (or pronouns) in time or space, or in metaphorical interpretations of temporal and spatial relationships. There are two types of prepositions found in Spanish: *simple* (one-word forms) and *compound*. Prepositional phrases, which are easily identified because they begin with a preposition, function both as adjectives and adverbs.

Simple forms

The following is a complete list of all the simple prepositions in Spanish. English and Spanish often use different prepositions for the same verb, as the example below the list shows.

a	*at, to*
ante	*before, in front of*
bajo*	*under, beneath*
con	*with*
contra	*against*
de	*of, from*
desde	*from, since*
durante	*during*
en	*in, into, at, on*
entre	*among, between*
excepto	*except*
hacia	*toward*
hasta	*until, to, up to*
mediante	*be means of*
para	*for, toward*
por	*for, by, through, along, around, around in, across, within*
salvo	*except, save for*
según	*according to*
sin	*without*
so	*under (now exclusively legal, e.g.,* so pena de—*under pain of)*
sobre	*on, about, concerning*
tras	*after*

***Bajo** is an adjective serving as a preposition.

59

El libro está **en** la mesa.	*The book is **on** the table.*
Juan no está **en** casa.	*John is not **at** home.*

Compound

Many of the compound prepositions are synonymous with some of the simple forms. The following list of useful, high-frequency expressions involving multiple prepositions is a starting point for your emerging mastery of compound prepositions. To perfect your skill in using these, note when you come across them in articles or when you hear them. In this way, you can distinguish the various situations in which one is more appropriate than another, whose dictionary meaning may be identical.

a causa de	*on account of*
a excepción de	*with the exception of*
a fuerza de	*by virtue/dint of*
a menos que	*unless*
a pesar de	*in spite of*
acerca de	*about, concerning*
además de	*besides, in addition to*
adversamente a	*adversely to*
alrededor de	*around*
antes de	*before (time, order)*
a través	*across*
con tal de que	*provided that*
concerniente a	*concerning*
conforme a	*according to*
congruente con	*consistent with*
contrario a	*contrary to*
correspondiente a	*corresponding to*
debajo de	*under, underneath, beneath*
delante de	*before (place), in front of*
dentro de	*within*
después de	*after (time, order)*
detrás de	*behind, after (place)*
encima de	*over, on top of*
en cuanto a	*as for*
en frente de	*in front of*
en vez de	*instead of*
en virtud de	*by virtue of*
frente a	*opposite to*
junto a	*close to*
lejos de	*far from*
por causa de	*on account of*
por razón de	*by reason of*
relativo a	*in relation to*
respecto a	*with respect to*
sin embargo	*notwithstanding*
tocante a	*in (or with) regard to*

La farmacia está **frente al** banco.	*The pharmacy is **opposite** the bank.*
Vamos al cine **en vez del** teatro.	*Let's go to the movies **instead of** the theater.*

Often, prepositional usage in Spanish makes perfect sense to English-speaking learners, but when it is baffling, it can be maddening. There are three major reasons for this. First, quite simply, people tend to take these words for granted—that is, they don't give them much thought, unless they are, for example, reading legal contracts or giving directions for assembling a piece of equipment.

Secondly, prepositional usage is confusing because learners are unaware of the way verbs are "built." Following are three common examples. **Casarse** and **soñarse** both require the preposition **con** to indicate the English *to get married to* and *to dream about*. **Enamorarse** requires **de** for the English *to fall in love with*. Consider how the use of **con** with **casarse** makes sense when you realize that the verb is built from the noun **casa** turned into the verb **casar** (*to house*). Then realize that when two people get married, they make their house *with* each other!

The third reason English speakers find Spanish prepositional usage baffling is that English has a vast number of phrasal verbs—verbs whose meaning changes completely depending on the preposition used with them. In the introduction, reference was made to these verbs. As a point of departure for exploring how these verbs complicate verb choice in Spanish, experiment with how the meanings of the English verbs *get* and *put* change radically by appending different prepositions to them. One of the exercises at the end of this chapter will expose you to a handful of common phrasal verbs involving *get* and *put*.

Since there are thousands of phrasal verbs in English, the best way to deal with the problem of learning their Spanish counterparts is to be careful when using a dictionary. If you want the proper Spanish verb to express *Get down!* (when this is meant as a warning of danger), you will find solutions in **bajarse** or **agacharse**, depending on the physical parameters of the situation.

Observe the following two examples. The first might be what a mother says to her son when he climbs too high in a tree. The second could happen on a battlefield, where the more likely English expression upon perceiving incoming fire would be "Duck!" and even more problematic if you looked in a dictionary and carelessly picked the noun for the bird.

¡**Bájate** de allí, Juanito!	*Get down from there, Johnny!*
¡Fuego! ¡**Agáchense**!	*Fire! Get down!*

Por and para

The pair of prepositions **por** and **para** cause English speakers more trouble than perhaps any other word pair in Spanish for which English has only one word. Let's begin at the most abstract level. **Para** is dynamic, as the following three examples show. In the first example, **para** is operating in a spatial way. The speaker is observing the flight of the plane as a vector—its flight path is in a certain direction. The second example shows **para** functioning in a temporal way, pointing toward a deadline. The third example simply shows that **para** is the preposition that must be used before an infinitive when you want to say *in order to*; that is, you cannot simply use the infinitive to do this as is possible in English and as is shown by the second translation of the third example.

El avión vuela **para** Alaska.	*The plane is flying to/toward/for Alaska.*
El artículo es **para** la edición de mañana.	*The article is for tomorrow's edition.*
Estudiamos español **para** poder hablarlo bien.	*We study Spanish in order to be able to speak it well.*
	We study Spanish to be able to speak it well.

The preposition **para** also is used to express an unexpected or surprise comparison. Observe the following examples.

Juanito sabe mucho de matemáticas **para** un niño de ocho años.	*Johnny knows a lot about math **for** a boy of eight.*
Para administrador, el Sr. Acero es bien bobo.	***For** an administrator, Mr. Acero is really dumb.*
¡Vaya!, **Para** un equipo de colegio, juegan como profesionales.	*Wow! **For** a high school team, they play like pros!*

The preposition **para** also shows the purpose for something:

Un martillo no sirve **para** eso.	*A hammer is no good for that.*
Es una copa **para** cognac.	*It is a cognac snifter.*

The preposition **por** is rendered in English by many prepositions, for instance: *through, around, within, by, along, per,* and of course, *for,* as in many stock phrases such as **por Dios** (*for the love of God*). You can see how many of these prepositions are used spatially simply by their meaning:

Caperucita Roja caminó **por** el bosque.	*Little Red Riding Hood walked through the forest.*
El perro corría **por** el río.	*The dog was running along the river.*

The preposition **por** can also be used in a figurative way, just as many of its English counterparts can.

Fue **por** sus estudios que llegó a ser médico.	*It was through his studies that he became a doctor.*

Now that you see how **por** works *spatially*, it will be easy to see that its *temporal* uses are analogous. For instance, one function of **por** is to show duration of time (e.g., **por tres días**). In comparison to **para**, **por** is static. The action of the verb with which **por** is associated takes place *across, along, around, by, in, through* or *within* some space where **por** is relating two nouns, as the following examples show.

Los novios caminaron **por** el parque por dos horas.	*The couple walked around in the park for two hours.*
El pájaro volaba **por** las ramas.	*The bird was flying around/amid/through/among the branches.*
Pasé **por** tu casa pero no estabas.	*I went by your house but you weren't there.*

By now, it should be becoming clear that the problem of **por** and **para** is best solved by concluding two things. First, the English preposition *for* is not used in one way—to mean one thing—in English, as the previous examples show. Second, **por** and **para** don't simply mean *for* (whatever meaning you wish to give it). Think about the following examples and substitute each of the English prepositions just cited, one at a time, and you'll see just how **por** works as a spatial preposition. Note that the two nouns being related in the first example are the *dog* and the *room*, and the preposition **por** shows how the dog's action happened in that space. English has some advantage over Spanish because English has a number of prepositions that can be more specific about the dog's movement with respect to the room.

El perro corrió **por** la sala.	*The dog ran around the room.*
Juan estuvo **por** aquí ayer a las tres.	*John was around here yesterday at three.*

As a temporal preposition, **por** means **during**, or *for* in the sense of *duration of time*. It also corresponds exactly to the uses of *per*, which is the Latin word it evolved from. Other meanings of **por** include *for the sake of* and *because*, when used in the sense of *on account of*. It is also used to mark a noun as the *object of an errand*. In addition, there are many, stock phrases using **por**, most of which will come easily.

Estuvimos en Guanajuato **por** varios días.	*We were in Guanajuato for a few days.*
No lo van a hacer, **por** ahora.	*They aren't going to do it, for now.*
El carro iba a cien kilómetros **por** hora.	*The car was traveling at a sixty miles an hour.*
Hidalgo murió **por** la Patria.	*Hidalgo died for the country.*

Por cobarde, no quiso contestarme.	*Because he's a coward, he refused to answer me.*
Mi hermana fue a la tienda **por** pan.	*My sister went to the shop for bread.*

But:

Mi hermana fue a la tienda **para** comprar pan.	*My sister went to the shop to buy bread.*

The differences between **por** and **para** account for why these two questions are so different:

¿Por qué quieres ser médico?	*Why do you want to be a physician?*
¿Para qué quieres ser médico?	*What [on earth] do you want to be a physician for?*

Finally, I offer you one final, general comment about prepositions. You may have heard it said that in English you shouldn't end a sentence (or a clause) with a preposition. First, that isn't so. Winston Churchill is often quoted (rightly or wrongly) for observing that such a rule was *a lot of poppycock up with which he would not put* (!). There is no such rule in English, as anyone can prove by picking up a volume of Shakespeare. However, in Spanish, it is an absolute rule. In Spanish, you must never end a sentence or clause with a preposition. Note the following examples.

No tengo **con quién** hablar allí.	*I have no one to speak with there.*
¿De quién fue la llamada?	*Who was the call from?*
¿De qué sabor es esto?	*What flavor is this (of)?*

EJERCICIO
8·1

Match the following English prepositions with their Spanish counterparts—remember, though, that usage is not as simple as matching them!

_____	1.	with	a.	en
_____	2.	against	b.	hacia
_____	3.	to, at	c.	sobre
_____	4.	close to	d.	a
_____	5.	under, underneath, beneath	e.	por
_____	6.	on, in, at	f.	hasta
_____	7.	on, about, concerning	g.	desde
_____	8.	with respect to	h.	entre
_____	9.	for, by, around	i.	contra
_____	10.	within	j.	frente a
_____	11.	of, from	k.	detrás de
_____	12.	from	l.	debajo de
_____	13.	opposite to	m.	tras
_____	14.	among, between	n.	respecto a

_____ 15. toward   o. con

_____ 16. after   p. lejos de

_____ 17. behind, after (place)   q. para

_____ 18. until   r. junto a

_____ 19. for, toward   s. dentro de

_____ 20. far from   t. de

EJERCICIO

8·2

*Match the following English phrasal verbs involving the verbs **get** and **put** with their corresponding Spanish solutions.*

_____ 1. to get even   a. casarse

_____ 2. to become (e.g., a doctor)   b. subir

_____ 3. to get bored   c. cansarse

_____ 4. to put on (e.g., clothes)   d. sobreponerse

_____ 5. to put up with   e. devolver

_____ 6. to get on (e.g., a bus)   f. enamorarse de

_____ 7. to put down (e.g., jot a note)   g. enfermarse

_____ 8. to get tired   h. aguantar

_____ 9. to get going   i. encarcelar

_____ 10. to get it (e.g., a joke).   j. aburrirse

_____ 11. to get over (e.g., a problem)   k. darse prisa

_____ 12. to put down (e.g., a personal affront)   l. extraviarse

_____ 13. to put back (e.g., an object)   m. vengarse

_____ 14. to get married   n. llegar a ser

_____ 15. to get sick   o. mejorarse

_____ 16. to fall in love with   p. apuntar

_____ 17. to put away (e.g., jail)   q. apagar

_____ 18. to get lost   r. ponerse

_____ 19. to put out (e.g., a fire)   s. insultar

_____ 20. to get better (e.g., from illness)   t. comprender

¿Por or para?

1. Le voy a ofrecer mil dólares _____ su auto.

2. El helicóptero pasó velozmente _____ encima del edificio sin chocar con nada.

3. El avión volaba a mil kilómetros _____ hora.

4. La niña fue a la tienda _____ arroz.

5. _____ esto he venido: ayudarte a pintar la casa.

6. El Sr. José Martí y el Dr. José Rizal dieron sus vidas _____ sus patrias.

7. Y, _____ colmo, el Sr. Acero es mentiroso.

8. ¿_____ qué no vamos a San Francisco de vacaciones?

9. A lo mejor, ese avión va _____ San Francisco.

10. Este regalo es _____ mi mamá.

11. Su amigo estaba enfermo, así que Juan asistió a la reunión _____ él.

12. Sé que dejé mi billetera _____ aquí.

13. Necesito el informe sobre la contaminación del río _____ el viernes.

14. Juan y Tomás iban al centro comercial _____ buscar un regalo.

15. Si quieres, amigo, yo se lo diré _____ respaldarte.

16. ¿_____ qué sirve esta herramienta?

17. El Sr. Acero debe ir a la cárcel _____ razón de su corrupción.

18. Te digo que fue _____ eso que no lo puedo ver ni en pintura.

19. Mi amigo estudió mucho _____ llegar a ser profesor.

20. Los novios pasaron una hora caminando _____ el parque.

Translate the following sentences from Spanish to English.

1. Esa familia pasaba por el pueblo en marzo todos los años.

   _____

2. Por poco, el héroe de guerra da la vida por la liberación de su país.

   _____

3. Debido a sus nociones limitadas sobre la política, yo intenté convencerle con las mías.

   _____

4. Las aguas se precipitaban por un lecho de piedras entre dos montañas.

   _____

5. Se fundó la aldea a orillas del río.

   _____

6. Un hombre se cayó por el techo cuando intentó robar la casa.

   _____

7. La anciana de pelo rizado enterró una figura llena de oro debajo de la cama.

   _____

8. Por dondequiera que fuera, se oía una música suave.

   _____

9. El hermano menor, con sus esfuerzos y talento, trabajó por años para arreglar la casa.

   _____

10. Llovió por varios días.

    _____

11. Un hombre subió al tren que no iba hacia ninguna parte, sin rumbo cierto ni destino.

    _____

12. La señora que vive en el piso de abajo fue la única que le tuvo lástima.

    _____

13. Los perros corrieron tras el conejo.

    _____

14. La ruta del correo de mulas pasaba por las montañas.

    _____

15. El músico estuvo sentado en medio de las piezas desarmadas de un clavicordio.

    _____

16. Las palomas, asustadas por el grito de la mujer, volaron hacia las nubes.

    _____

17. Debido a su locura, varios hombres lo tuvieron que refrenar con cuerdas.

    _____

18. La lanza que arrojó el héroe voló hasta que pasó por el pecho del general enemigo.

    _____

19. El acusado tuvo que comparecer ante el juez.

_____

20. La ciudad se hundió en el lodo.

_____

Translate the following sentences from English to Spanish.

1. The dog almost ran under the bus.

_____

2. The house is within five miles of the city.

_____

3. Mr. Acero made accusations not only without evidence but contrary to it.

_____

4. He didn't tell us anything about it.

_____

5. She got angry with him when he came into the house.

_____

6. When I left the movie, I saw the girl I had fallen in love with.

_____

7. She told me that she dreamed about me.

_____

8. They weren't sure if they should get married or not.

_____

9. The story, according to which he was from Italy, turned out to be false.

_____

10. The children ran through the house, getting mud all over the carpet.

_____

11. Don't betray the king, under pain of death! (**Ud.**)

_____

12. They looked until they found everything they wanted to sell.

_____

13. As for me, give me Liberty or give me Death. (**tú**)

_____

14. Not withstanding their differences, they agreed to sign the treaty.

_____

15. Whose book is this?

_____

16. Instead of complaining, you should work. (**tú**)

_____

17. The library is close to the building I work in.

_____

18. Does she expect to speak with him?

_____

19. Despite what she said, she is interested in him.

_____

20. They marched across the desert.

_____

_____

The preterit and imperfect tenses

The two single-word, or *simple* past tenses in Spanish confuse English-speaking learners for two main reasons. The first is conceptual: English has only one single-word past tense. Many English speakers have difficulty recognizing that English has various verbal constructions that correspond neatly to the functions of the imperfect in Spanish. The second reason is morphological, or form-related: many high-frequency verbs have new stems in their preterit forms and their irregularities bear no resemblance to the irregular patterns found in the present tense. The **preterit** and the **imperfect** are both past tenses—but they reflect two different, and often subjective, perceptions of past action. The preterit and the imperfect have split the reporting of past actions between them. They are not interchangeable.

The existence of these two aspects of the past is truly an elegant feature of the language, making its telling about the past vivid and clear. Furthermore, the fact that there are only three irregular verbs in the imperfect eases some of the burden, allowing you to concentrate on first learning the forms of verbs in the preterit and then to manage these two tenses, whether used alone or together. Let's start with the imperfect.

The imperfect

The imperfect is usually the first past tense taught after the present indicative. Aside from having different endings on the verbs, this tense differs from the present tense in two ways. First, rather than having three conjugation patterns for each of the three families of verbs (-**ar**, -**er**, and -**ir**), the imperfect indicative has two: one for -**ar** verbs and one in common for the -**er** and -**ir** verbs. Secondly, the first- and third-person singular forms are identical for all verbs in the imperfect, whether regular or irregular. This means that the subject pronouns must be used more often, in order to avoid ambiguity.

The three verbs that are irregular in the imperfect are **ir**, **ser**, and **ver**. From an historical perspective, it could be said that **ver** is not irregular. Once upon a time, it was spelled **veer** and thus similar to **leer**, whose conjugation in the imperfect looks exactly the same, except for the first letter. Note that the **nosotros** and **vosotros** forms of **ir** and **ser** are stressed on their first syllable, as indicated by the accent mark:

IR		SER		VER	
iba	íbamos	era	éramos	veía	veíamos
ibas	ibais	eras	erais	veías	veíais
iba	iban	era	eran	veía	veían

The preterit

As far as regular verbs are concerned, the preterit, just as the imperfect, has one set of endings for the -**ar** verbs and another set in common for the -**er** and -**ir** verbs. However, from a morphological perspective, the preterit presents a challenge because of the many irregular verbs and the different types of irregularities, but this challenge can be managed by classifying the irregular verbs by type of irregularity and then grouping them by ending. Before dealing with that task, let's examine the three model regular verbs **hablar**, **comer**, and **vivir** to see how the majority of verbs in Spanish are conjugated in the preterit:

HABLAR		COMER		VIVIR	
hablé	hablamos	comí	comimos	viví	vivimos
hablaste	hablasteis	comiste	comisteis	viviste	vivisteis
habló	hablaron	comió	comieron	vivió	vivieron

The regular pattern of the preterit includes the fact that the first-person plural of both -**ar** and -**ir** verbs is identical to their present indicative forms and that the final vowel of the first- and third-person singular forms is stressed as shown by the written accent mark. This last detail is very important because, for instance, **hablo** means *I speak*, but **habló** can mean *he, she,* or *you* (formal, singular) *spoke*. The only constant morphological feature across the whole verb system is that -**mos** and -**n** are the person and number markers for **nosotros** and the third-person plural, respectively.

Now let's tackle the irregular verbs. The verbs that are irregular in the preterit can be divided into five groups, at least three of which are easy to deal with and have the same endings as they would if they were regular. These three groups that comprise irregular verbs with regular endings are as follows:

- verbs with stem-vowel changes
- verbs with a consonant change in their **yo** form to preserve pronunciation of the final consonant in the infinitive
- verbs with an orthographical convention wherein i → y when -i- falls between vowels

I call the fourth group of irregular preterit verbs the "tough crowd" because they involve completely new stems and have their own set of endings. The fifth group involves **dar**, **ser**, and **ir**, whose irregularities don't allow them to fit into the fourth group.

In the first easy group, we find those verbs that, in the present indicative, have a stem vowel irregularity of **e → i** (e.g., **pedir**, **servir**, and **repetir**) and only two verbs (**dormir** and **morir**) with a stem vowel change of **o → ue**. In the preterit, however, the **e → i** change *only* occurs in the third-person, both singular and plural. In the verbs **morir** and **dormir**, whose vowel stem change in the present indicative is **o → ue**, the vowel change in the preterit is **o → u**, and also *only* in the third-person singular and plural.

PEDIR		DORMIR	
pedí	pedimos	dormí	dorminos
pediste	pedisteis	dormiste	dormisteis
pidió	pidieron	durmió	durmieron

The next easy group includes all verbs whose infinitives end in -**car**, -**gar**, and -**zar** (e.g., **buscar**, **pagar**, and **empezar**). These verbs are regular in pronunciation, but undergo a spelling change in the **yo** form in order to conform to the spelling conventions used to represent those sounds.

BUSCAR		PAGAR		EMPEZAR	
busqué	buscamos	pagué	pagamos	empecé	empezamos
buscaste	buscasteis	pagaste	pagasteis	empezaste	empezasteis
buscó	buscaron	pagó	pagaron	empezó	empezaron

The last easy group also involves a spelling change only, and again in the third-person singular and plural. It consists of all verbs whose infinitive ends in -**uir** (e.g., **construir**), the verb **leer**, and any other verb or word whose morphology would place an -i- between two vowels. This slight irregularity is merely in response to a spelling rule of relatively recent date that says that whenever the letter -i- falls between two other vowels in the same word, it must be changed to a -y-. You will recall analogous situations where the conjunction **y** (*and*) also changes to an **e** before words beginning with **i**- or **hi**- and **o** (*or*) changes to **u** before words beginning with **o**- or **ho**-.

CONSTRUIR		LEER	
construí	construimos	leí	leímos
construiste	construisteis	leíste	leísteis
construyó	construyeron	leyó	leyeron

The fourth group of irregular preterit verbs is that "tough crowd," and consists of the verbs upon whom new stems are bestowed for their preterit forms (and, consequently, for their imperfect subjunctive forms). In addition, these verbs share their own common set of endings in the preterit, regardless of whether they are -**ar**, -**er**, or -**ir** verbs. The good news is that there are fewer than twenty high-frequency verbs to deal with, and these can be grouped according to the final stem consonants or the last vowel and consonant of their new stems, creating a rhyme. Since the new stems are used in all three persons, singular and plural, and since you need to memorize the first-person singular of the preterit, the following list shows the **yo** form of these high-frequency verbs.

andar	anduve	saber	supe	decir	dije
estar	estuve	caber	cupe	conducir	conduje
tener	tuve	reproducir	reproduje		
		traducir	traduje		
		traer	traje		

Verbs whose preterit stem ends in a -**j** drop the **i** of the third-person preterit ending (e.g., **trajeron**; compare this with the conjugation of **tener**).

The new stem of the verb **haber** almost rhymes with those of **saber** and **caber**, but it is so important for forming the pluperfect subjunctive (as the helping verb) that it should be memorized separately. Finally, the new stems of **querer** and **hacer** do rhyme, but only in the Americas, due to the pronunciation of **ce** and **ci** in much of Spain.

haber	→hube	poner	→puse
		poder	→pude
querer	→quise	hacer	→hice

The set of common endings which all these "new" stem verbs have is exemplified by the following conjugation of **tener**. Note that unlike regular verbs or even the verbs with minor spelling changes in their preterit stems, the first- and third-persons singular of the endings of the tough crowd are *not* accented.

TENER

tuve	tuvimos
tuviste	tuvisteis
tuvo	tuvieron

The fifth and last group of irregular preterit verbs is made up of the three verbs whose preterit forms are irregular and do not fit into the "tough crowd." They are, as mentioned at the beginning of this section, **dar**, **ser**, and **ir**. The good news is that **ser** and **ir** are identical and **dar** is conjugated as if it were a regular **-ir** verb. Their final syllables are not stressed either.

DAR		**SER**		**IR**	
di	dimos	fui	fuimos	fui	fuimos
diste	disteis	fuiste	fuisteis	fuiste	fuisteis
dio	dieron	fue	fueron	fue	fueron

Imperfect or preterit?

Having dealt with the forms of the imperfect and the preterit, you are now ready to observe how these two aspects of the past are used. Among teachers and students, there are many, many analogies, explanations, and mnemonic acronyms to help students conceptualize the use of these two tenses. So this is the proper moment to start at the conceptual level with the broadest, one-word label for what each of these tenses is about and then begin narrowing it:

- ◆ The imperfect is descriptive.
- ◆ The preterit is narrative.

When we say that the imperfect is *descriptive*, we refer to its role in setting a stage and giving background information about how a situation was. It is *not* used to tell what happened, but rather for telling what was going on or how things appeared, what conditions were. This is why time of day and one's age are always expressed in the imperfect. Weather phenomena in the past (what the day was like), are also expressed in the imperfect (unless you're telling about some phenomenon starting or stopping, or summing it up—functions of the preterit). Time is always flowing, and the imperfect reflects that in all its usages. The imperfect invites amplification and detail in terms of action—but that is the function reserved for the preterit. Consider the imperfect as you would stage directions that tell a set designer what to build and where to place items on a stage. The action is what goes on there. When the imperfect is used, one is in the middle of that flow, not at its beginning or end.

César **era** dictador.	*Caesar was a dictator.*
Era un día claro y hacía sol.	*It was a clear, sunny day.*
Mi tía **tenía** seis años en esta foto.	*My aunt was six years old in this photo.*
Eran las cuatro de la tarde...	*It was four in the afternoon . . .*

By contrast, and as its complement, the preterit is *narrative*. It tells or summarizes what happened at a particular moment. The preterit is used to tell when actions started and ended, and, when it summarizes, it can enclose even long periods of time. It treats time as an expandable or contractible parenthesis.

El siglo diecinueve **fue** el siglo de la clase media.	*The nineteenth century was the century of the middle class.*

Compare the following sentences. The first is in the preterit and the second in the imperfect.

Dejó de llover.	*It stopped raining.*
Dejaba de llover.	*The rain was letting up.*

The Spanish imperfect is almost always used when English uses *were + gerund (-ing)* to express an action already in progress or as *used to + verb*, to express habitual or repeated actions in the past. It also is used whenever *would + verb* can be substituted for *used to + verb*—but beware: it is *not* used in any other instances where *would + verb* is used in English. The other uses of *would* in English will require either the *conditional* or the *imperfect subjunctive*, when the English use of *would* is anticipatory. If you remember these observations as well as the use of the imperfect for time of day and telling a person's age in the past, then you'll be right more than 90 percent of the time.

The following examples illustrate uses of *would* with different Spanish tenses.

Cuando era niño, **jugaba** con mi perro.	*When I was a boy, I would play with my dog.*
Ella esperaba que Juan le **pidiera** la mano.	*She was hoping that John would ask her to marry him.*
Si tuviera más tiempo libre, lo **pasaría** con mi hija.	*If I had more free time, I would spend it with my daughter.*

As for the preterit's equivalent in English, the general rule of thumb is that it is used when English uses a simple, one-word past tense. But this rule is not as reliable as the observations about when the imperfect is used, particularly where the verb *to be* is used in English (**ser** and **estar** in Spanish) or when the action of the verb is qualified in some way by an adverb. Compare the following two sentences, the first of which is in the preterit, the second in the imperfect. These two sentences alone should suffice to demonstrate that often, the choice between using the preterit or the imperfect is not a matter of grammar, but rather of what one intends to communicate.

Fuimos a la playa.	*We went to the beach.*
Íbamos a la playa mucho.	*We went to the beach a lot.*

Now let's examine four verbs that, when used in the preterit, do not mean what the dictionary typically gives as the primary meaning of their infinitive forms. These verbs are **saber** and **conocer**—the two verbs that mean *to know* (but in very different senses)—and the auxiliary verbs **querer** (*to want*) and **poder** (*to be able*). Since the preterit focuses on a moment in time when an action occurs, these verbs are used in the preterit to mean, respectively, *to find out*, *to meet*, *to try* (or, in the negative, *to refuse*) and *to succeed* (or, in the negative, *to fail*). When their primary meanings are needed in the past, the imperfect is used. Observe the following contrastive examples.

¿Cuándo **supiste** que él falsificó la documentación?	*When did you find out that he falsified the documents?*
Yo ya **sabía** que el tipo era mentiroso.	*I already knew the guy was a liar.*
Yo **conocí** a la francesa en una fiesta.	*I met the French woman at a party.*
Goethe **conocía** bien la ópera *Die Zauberflöte*.	*Goethe was very familiar with the opera Die Zauberflöte.*
Ellos **quisieron** abrir la caja fuerte.	*They tried to open the safe.*
No **quería** que nadie descubriera su crimen.	*He didn't want anyone to discover his crime.*

Por fin, **pude** escalar la montaña.
No la **pudieron** abrir.
En el colegio, Juan no **podía** correr
tan rápido como su hermano.

Finally, I succeeded at scaling the mountain.
They failed to open it.
In high school, John couldn't run as fast as his
brother.

The glorious thing about these two aspects of the past is their ability to create vivid verbal cinema. Examine the following sentences in light of what this chapter has observed about how they conceptualize action in the past.

El intruso **abría** la ventana con
cuidado y mientras **observaba** al
señor que **leía**, no **advirtió** que éste
ocultaba un revólver ya armado en
su regazo.

The thief opened the window cautiously
and, as he observed the gentleman
reading, he failed to notice that the fellow
was hiding in his lap a revolver already
cocked.

Me **dijeron** que **sabían** que el galeón
estaba a docenas de metros debajo
de la superficie del mar, pero que
quisieron subirlo porque **había**
varios millones de dólares en
piezas de a ocho en el suelo
submarino.

They told me they knew the galleon was
dozens of meters below the surface, but
they tried to raise it, because there was
several millions of dollars' worth of pieces
of eight on the sea floor.

Cuando **supe** lo que el Sr. Acero me
hacía, **decidí** denunciarlo ante
todos.

When I found out what Mr. Acero was
doing to me, I decided to denounce him
before all.

Mientras **conversaban** en el pasillo
sobre los pasteles que **horneaban**
los fines de semana, yo **seguí**
escribiendo.

While they chatted in the hallway about the
cakes they were baking on weekends, I
kept writing.

The following exercises will test your ability to properly conjugate verbs in the imperfect and preterit, as well as to determine which form to use in various contexts.

EJERCICIO
9·1

Give the proper form of the verb in the imperfect, according to the subject pronoun in
parentheses.

1. (él) mirar _____

2. (tú) comer _____

3. (Ud.) tener _____

4. (yo) ver _____

5. (nosotros) haber _____

6. (ellas) hacer _____

7. (vosotros) trabajar _____

8. (yo) querer _____

9. (ellos) poder _____

10. (Uds.) deber _____

11. (ella) ser _____

12. (Ud.) ver _____

13. (tú) ir _____

14. (yo) poder _____

15. (él) ser _____

16. (ella) ir _____

17. (Uds.) establecer _____

18. (nosotros) leer _____

19. (yo) escribir _____

20. (tú) creer _____

Give the proper form of the verb in the preterit, according to the subject pronoun in parentheses.

1. (yo) ver _____

2. (tú) sentir _____

3. (Ud.) saber _____

4. (ellos) caber _____

5. (yo) dar _____

6. (ella) viajar _____

7. (Uds.) vivir _____

8. (yo) traer _____

9. (nosotros) trabajar _____

10. (ella) querer _____

11. (yo) entretener _____

12. (tú) conducir _____

13. (yo) tener _____

14. (vosotros) haber _____

15. (ellos) hablar _____

16. (yo) poner _____

17. (ella) estar _____

18. (tú) comer _____

19. (ellos) poder _____

20. (tú) hacer _____

EJERCICIO

9·3

Translate the following sentences from Spanish to English.

1. Mientras mis hermanas hablaban, yo tocaba la guitarra.

   _____

2. Cuando salió la película *La guerra de las galaxias*, yo tenía 22 años.

   _____

3. Había varios hombres en la esquina cuando el auto se resbaló y se chocó contra la pared.

   _____

4. Cuando estábamos de vacaciones, mis amigos y yo esquiábamos e íbamos a restaurantes.

   _____

5. ¿Dónde estabas tú y qué hacías cuando ocurrió el eclipse total de sol?

   _____

6. Comimos, descansamos y miramos la tele un rato, luego decidimos ir a la playa.

   _____

7. No me gustó cuando preparaba la cena y sonó el teléfono.

   _____

8. Los niños jugaban en el patio cuando llegó la abuela.

   _____

9. Se despertaba Elena cuando su papá llamó.

   _____

10. Eran las cuatro de la tarde y llovía cuando salí del cine.

   _____

11. Mi hermana tenía cuatro años cuando nací.

   _____

12. ¿Qué tiempo hacía cuando iban al lago para esquiar?

_____

13. Mis padres se mudaron a otra casa cuando yo tenía dos años.

_____

14. El perro se echó a correr tras el conejo tan pronto como lo vio.

_____

15. A las tres en punto estuve esperando en la entrada de la biblioteca.

_____

16. Cuando dejó de llover, regresamos a la carpa.

_____

17. La cena salió bien ya que la comida estuvo rica.

_____

18. Ese año, nevó mucho en la ciudad.

_____

19. Cuando me di cuenta de que no tenía acceso a la red, decidí marcharme.

_____

20. La banda tocaba y la gente bailaba, pero me sentía solo.

_____

_____

EJERCICIO
9·4

Translate the following sentences from English to Spanish.

1. When I arrived, the dog was sleeping.

_____

2. While you were eating, our brother was working. (**tú**)

_____

3. She left when he arrived.

_____

4. Alexandra was three years old when we moved to Seattle.

_____

5. After we got in the taxi, it began to rain.

_____

6. Yesterday was a very cold day for Seattle.

_____

7. He was fixing the table when he hurt his hand.

_____

8. Were you trying to call me yesterday? (**tú**)

_____

9. It was five in the afternoon, and raining, when my friends decided to come to visit me.

_____

10. I was preparing roast beef while I wrote this exercise.

_____

11. While I was setting the table, my friend was downstairs packing for his trip.

_____

12. Three birds were sitting on a wire when, suddenly, the cat tried to climb up to eat one.

_____

13. Her mother sat down when she heard the news.

_____

14. Mr. Acero was gossiping, everyone was listening to him, but only a few believed him.

_____

15. She wanted to go to bed but had too much work due the next day.

_____

16. The plane landed while it was snowing.

_____

17. When the train stopped, the passengers got off.

_____

18. While the ship was coming into port, customs agents detained it.

_____

19. While my grandmother knitted, we and the dog would play.

_____

20. Her friends bought her the gift while she was eating lunch.

_____

Preterit or imperfect? Fill in the blanks with the proper form of the verbs in parentheses.

Cuando Juan y María (1) _____ (ser) pequeños todavía, su familia (2) _____ (vivir) en el campo. Un día, su papá (3) _____ (aceptar) un puesto con una compañía extranjera que le (4) _____ (exigir) mudarse a Chile. Aunque su esposa no (5) _____ (saber) hablar español, a ella le (6) _____ (parecer) una muy buena e importante oportunidad para que los hijos lo aprendieran. Así que ella (7) _____ (aceptar) la idea con entusiasmo.

Mientras ellos (8) _____ (prepararse) para la mudanza y (9) _____ (hacer) las maletas y (10) _____ (empacar) todo, le (11) _____ (llegar) los boletos de avión. Juan y María (12) _____ (alegrarse) mucho porque nunca habían volado.

(13) _____ (Llegar) el día tan esperado. (14) _____ (Llover) cuando la familia (15) _____ (salir) de casa, pero todos (16) _____ (estar) muy contentos porque (17) _____ (ir) a tener una experiencia agradable: un viaje en avión y una nueva casa en otro país. (18) _____ (Ser) las ocho de la noche cuando ellos (19) _____ (abordar) el avión. Ellos (20) _____ (tener) que hacer muchas escalas—en México, D.F., en Panamá y en Lima. Cuando por fin el último vuelo (21) _____ (aterrizar) en Santiago, ellos (22) _____ (bajar) del avión y los niños (23) _____ (sorprenderse) porque (24) _____ (hacer) calor. ¡Las estaciones (25) _____ (estar) al revés y (26) _____ (ser) invierno en Estados Unidos!

Confusing verb pairs

Ser and estar

Intermediate-level students have the most difficulty distinguishing the differences in the usage of many pairs of verbs. The first verb pair they encounter, and the most notorious, is **ser** vs. **estar**, a pair of verbs that truly has only one English counterpart, the verb *to be*. The other confusing pairs often have alternative English translations that turn out to be better than the first-level dictionary entries. The mental hand-wringing over the other confusing verb pairs is often a result of not digging a bit deeper, as you will see. First, let's deal head-on with **ser** and **estar**.

The verb pair of **ser** and **estar** can be treated under three main subdivisions. In the majority of cases, which I call the 90 percent rule, **estar** is used for health and location and **ser** is used for everything else. If you understand and remember these two uses of **estar**, you can save yourself the trouble of having to memorize the uses of **ser**, although it is still useful and important to review them. There is only one use of **ser** that seems to contradict the use of **estar** for dealing with location. The verb **ser** is used to speak of where an event takes place. Most students find it helpful to consider this an example of *identifying* a location rather than saying where that place is (as in an address), as the last three examples show if you read them as a short dialogue.

¿Cómo **estás**?	*How are you?*
Mi oficina **está** en la ciudad.	*My office is in the city.*
¿Dónde **es** la fiesta de María?	*Where is Mary's party?*
Es en casa de José.	*It's at Joe's house.*
¿Dónde **está** la casa de José?	*Where is Joe's house?*

Let's review what is meant when I say that **ser** is used for "everything else." The verb **ser** is used to *identify* a person, place, thing, abstraction, and so forth. Thus, it is the verb needed to identify a person's profession, nationality, race, and religion. It is also used with **de** to show origin, material composition (what something is made of), and possession, corresponding to the English use of *apostrophe + s*. (Note that English uses an indefinite article in the following examples, but Spanish does not.)

Juan **es** médico.	*John is a doctor.*
Elena **es** estudiante.	*Helen is a student.*
Patricio **es** irlandés.	*Patrick is Irish.*
Iván **es** de Rusia.	*Ivan is from Russia.*
Mi suéter **es** de lana.	*My sweater is made of wool.*
Estos libros **son** de mi hermano.	*These books are my brother's.*

The second subdivision involves the use of both **ser** and **estar** as auxiliary or helping verbs. The use of the verb **estar** as a helping verb is often introduced early in many textbooks as the verb that, used with the gerund of another verb, forms the progressive aspect. In English, the progressive is also formed with the *be* verb, plus the English gerund, easily recognized as the *-ing* form. The endings **-ando** (for **-ar** verbs) and **-iendo** (for **-er/-ir** verbs) correspond to the *-ing* form of English, insofar as these are used to form the progressive. Note that the progressive is not used as much in Spanish as it is in English.

The progressive is used in Spanish when one emphasizes the immediacy of an ongoing action (in any tense). If used in the wrong circumstance, it can communicate a sense of urgency that the English usage does not communicate in the same circumstance.

Mi caballo **está cojeando**.	*My horse is limping.*
Esta tarde a las tres, **estaré preparando** la cena.	*This afternoon at three, I will be fixing dinner.*

Now consider this phone conversation. In English, the progressive is used quite routinely. However, if the progressive is used in Spanish, its use would communicate a sense of urgency.

Hola. ¿Qué **estás haciendo**?	*Hi. What are you doing (right now)?*
No mucho, pero, ¿qué pasa?	*Not much, but what's wrong?*

To avoid misunderstandings like this, simply use the present: **¿Qué haces?** This conveys no sense of urgency, as when English speakers casually ask *What are you doing?*

The passive voice

The verb **ser** is used to form the passive voice, which is not used nearly as much in Spanish as it is in English. Most verbs form their passive participles, also known as past participles, quite regularly. The **-ar** verbs drop the infinitive ending and append **-ado** and the **-er** and **-ir** verbs drop their infinitive endings and add **-ido**.

hablar	→hablado
comer	→comido
vivir	→vivido

However, there are a handful of common verbs whose passive participles are irregular:

abrir	abierto	morir	muerto
absolver	absuelto	poner	puesto
cubrir	cubierto	romper	roto
decir	dicho	ver	visto
escribir	escrito	volver	vuelto
hacer	hecho		

Another handful of verbs has two endings: the passive participle, formed regularly and used with **haber** to form the perfect tenses, and an irregular adjectival function. These verbs are:

	VERBAL	ADJECTIVAL
bendecir	bendecido	bendito
confesar	confesado	confeso
convertir	convertido	converso
elegir	elegido	electo
expresar	expresado	expreso
freír	freído	frito
imprimir	imprimido	impreso
reducir	reducido	reducto
suspender	suspendido	suspenso

The following examples contrast the use of the passive and active voice, which is preferred for most situations in Spanish as well as the **se** construction. Spanish frequently employs the **se** construction, also commonly called the pseudo-passive, instead of the true passive voice.

As the following examples show, the active voice reflects the reality in which a subject performs an action, while the passive voice makes the object of the action a grammatical subject and turns the "real" subject into a passive player in the sentence (using the preposition *by*). The **se** construction focuses solely on the action and does not mention the real world subject at all. In addition, note that the passive voice requires the agreement of the participle with its grammatical subject, since it is a *predicate adjective*. It helps to remember that the term *participle* indicates that it sometimes *participates* as a verb, sometimes as an adjective. The last example shows the passive participle in its role as an adjective (i.e., when it is not being used in passive constructions).

Active voice:

Los niños **rompieron** las ventanas.	*The boys broke the windows.*
Él **escribió** la novela.	*He wrote the novel.*

Passive voice:

Las ventanas **fueron rotas** por los niños.	*The windows were broken by the boys.*
La novela **fue escrita** por él.	*The novel was written by him.*

Se construction:

Se rompieron las ventanas.	*The windows broke/got broken.*
Se escribió la novela.	*The novel was written.*

Use with adjectives

The third subdivision regarding the usage of **ser** and **estar** deals with the use of these verbs with adjectives. There is one very mistaken idea that I would not mention were it not for the fact that it does not seem to go away in the world of Spanish teaching and learning. I refer to the notion that "**ser** is used with permanent characteristics and **estar** is used with temporary ones." This is misleading and simply not true. Consider the following examples. Their meanings prove the foregoing "rule" to be false:

Jacob Marley **está muerto**.	Jacob Marley is dead.
Juan **es soltero**.	John is single.
María **está casada**.	Mary is married.

Obviously, death is plenty permanent and yet **estar** is the proper verb to use. Then again, although marriages can end in death or divorce, **estar** once again is the proper verb to use when describing someone with regard to these characteristics. It might seem as if the often repeated but incorrect rule has something of a ring of truth about it and the examples above must simply be exceptions, but it is simply missing something important—almost everything changes over time. Over-thinking the choice of verb and trying to use this misleading notion will bring on headaches—and mistakes in Spanish (some of which can be humorous or embarrassing).

Compared with English, Spanish has fewer pure adjectives. The lack is made up by using passive participles, often with **estar** or **tener**. In the following examples, observe how the participles agree with the nouns they modify.

Las tres cartas, **escritas** en español, están en la mesa.	*The three letters, written in Spanish, are on the table.*
Mi tío tenía dos carros, **hechos** en el Japón.	*My uncle had two cars, made in Japan.*

Ser is used with characterizing adjectives when those adjectives describe something or someone in a normative or identifying way, such as one's physical features, social and economic status, and nationality.

Ellos **son** italianos.	*They are Italians.*
El Sr. Acero **es** mentiroso.	*Mr. Acero is a liar.*
Su hermano **es** comilón.	*His brother is a big eater.*
La nieve **es** blanca.	*Snow is white.*
Juanita **es** pelirroja.	*Jane is a redhead.*
Esos atletas **son** altos y fuertes.	*Those athletes are tall and strong.*

By over-thinking the problem, I refer to the fact that people can change their nationality or their character, habits, or hair color. Snow on the street turns black. Tall athletes will probably not lose much in the way of height over time, but there will come a day when they no longer will be considered robust. Yet the adjectives are considered normative, characterizing and identifying features of the subjects, and therefore **ser** will be used when the adjectives are meant to point to these features as identifying marks.

The verb **estar** is used with adjectives intending to show a *change of state or condition*. In fact, the word *state* derives from the same Latin root as the Spanish verb **estar**, a fact that might help you remember what follows. Thus, when we say **María está casada**, we are showing that the civil status she was born with (single) has changed; it also explains why **ser** is used when we say someone is single—that is everyone's civil status until they change it. Thus:

Juan **es** soltero.	*John is single.*
Ella **está** divorciada.	*She is divorced.*

Now let's consider some other examples of normal usage that are often a bit more challenging: social and economic status, and life and death.

Los gladiadores **están** muertos.	*The gladiators are dead. (the resultant state of combat)*
La Sra. Martínez **es** viuda.	*Mrs. Martínez is a widow. (her social condition)*

But if one says . . .

La Sra. Martínez **está** viuda (ahora).	*Mrs. Martinez is a widow (now).*

. . . it is because her husband has just died and the speaker is showing this recent change of her status. How long will the same speaker use **estar** when describing Mrs. Martínez as a widow? Until he or she comes to think of Mrs. Martínez's new social condition as a settled matter.

The verb **estar** is also used to indicate surprise or an unexpected observation. Imagine the following examples to be about a customer's reaction to the soup in a restaurant. The difference between using this verb and **ser** is that, with **estar**, the speaker is not expecting the soup to be as good as it is; when **ser** is used, he is reporting what he has come to know habitually.

¡La sopa **está** rica!	*The soup is delicious!*
La sopa **es** rica.	*The soup is delicious.*

This usage can also be applied to people. In the next example, imagine that the speaker is an older relative of a young boy whom she has not seen for a couple of years. She shows her surprise at how tall he is. Certainly, his height is not going to revert to what she remembers—the use of **estar** is simply to register her surprise. Soon, she will settle into using **ser** to describe this characteristic.

¡Ay, Jaimito, pero qué grande **estás**!	*Oh my, Jimmy, but how you've grown!*

Now for life and death:

Soy vivo.	*I am alive (as in I am a living person).* or *I am sharp (quick-witted).*

Likewise:

Es un muerto.	*He's a dead man.*

In the previous example, the speaker is identifying someone (a male) as a dead person (i.e., he is among the dead). Watch out though, because in some situations, this is a death threat! Certainly it would be if one said **¡Eres hombre muerto!**, or **¡Eres muerto/a!** You are a dead man/woman!

But what of this next example?

Estoy vivo.	*I'm alive.*

You would say this if something had threatened that condition, even if you're being humorous, after having a rough day at the office, for instance. It can be used in the same situations as when in English one says "I'm hanging in there".

Finally, some adjectives are used with either **ser** or **estar**—but their meaning changes as a consequence of that choice. Consider these examples:

Juan **está** casado.	*John is married. (a mere observation of his civil status—without any implications at all)*
Juan **es** casado.	*John is a married guy. (he doesn't cheat on his wife)*
Marta **está** cansada.	*Martha is tired.*
Marta **es** cansada.	*Martha is boring.*
El viejo **está** enfermo.	*The old man is sick.*
El viejo **es** enfermo.	*The old man is sickly.*
Juan, **¡estás** loco!	*John, you've lost your mind!*
Julio **es** loco.	*Julio is a crazy guy (the life of the party).*

Finally, many students find the problem of choosing between **ser** and **estar** compounded when they also face the choice of preterit vs. imperfect. Use the preterit of **estar** when a *specific* time frame or clock time is mentioned. In all other cases, if **estar** is the proper choice, then you'll need the imperfect.

¿Dónde **estabas** cuando te llamé?	*Where were you when I called?*
Estaba de compras cuando me llamaste.	*I was out shopping when you called.*
Ellos **estuvieron** en el museo por tres horas.	*They were in the museum for three hours.*
Estuve trabajando tres días sin dormir.	*I was working for three days without sleep.*
Fui a buscarte en la tienda a las tres pero no estuviste.	*I went to the shop to pick you up at three but you weren't there.*

In some regional varieties of Spanish, the last example would use **estabas**—which suggests that using the imperfect of **estar** is admissible, even when a time in the past is explicitly stated. Technically, however, this usage is an example of what is known as a *native error*.

As for other verb pairs that can cause confusion because they are often translated as one English verb, try finding another English verb to reflect each verb's peculiar nuance. Most problems either will not happen at all or will disappear quickly and quietly.

Saber and conocer

The verb pair **saber** vs. **conocer** deals with *to know*, but in what sense? **Saber** is *to have knowledge of, to possess a command of facts or a body of information*, while **conocer** is *to have familiarity with*, or *to be acquainted with a person, place, or ideas*.

Conozco bien la ciudad de Seattle.	*I know Seattle well.*
Quisiera conocer mejor las obras de Espronceda.	*I'd like to know Espronceda's works better.*
No la **conozco** a ella.	*I don't know her.*
Ella **sabe** la letra de todas las canciones populares.	*She knows the lyrics of all the pop tunes.*

In the preterit, **saber** means *to find out* and **conocer** means *to meet*—not because of anything peculiar about the verbs but because the preterit views past action as an event at a point in time in the past. Hence, if one compresses the notion of knowing facts to a moment, it focuses upon the moment when they became found out. Likewise, if being familiar with someone is compressed to a moment in the past, it can only refer to the moment when the two people met.

¿**Conociste** a mi hermano en el baile?	*Did you meet my brother at the dance?*
Cuando **supe** lo que el Sr. Acero había hecho, puse el grito en el cielo.	*When I found out what Mr. Acero had done, I hit the ceiling.*

Additionally, the verb **saber**, when followed by the preposition **a**, means to taste like:

Esto **sabe** a canela.	*This tastes like cinnamon.*

Finally, **saber** may be a helping verb. Followed by an infinitive, it means *to know how to do something*. Note that **cómo** is *not* used, although many native speakers of Spanish, if they have been contaminated by English, will often use it. It is proper to use **cómo** when asking how something is done.

Ella **sabe** tocar el piano.	*She knows how to play the piano.*
¿**Sabes** cómo se abre esta lata de anchoas?	*Do you know how to open this can of anchovies?*

Pedir and preguntar

The verb pair **pedir** and **preguntar** causes confusion only because they are too often introduced as meaning *to ask*. Instead, **pedir** means *to ask for* and **preguntar** means *to ask a question*. The whole muddle could be avoided from the outset if **pedir** is introduced as meaning *to request* or *to order* and **preguntar** as meaning *to question*. Interestingly, in Spanish there is no simple verb for *to borrow*, but rather **pedir prestado** (*to ask for something to be lent*).

Después de leer el menú, **pedí** langosta y una copa de champán.	*After reading the menu, I ordered lobster and a glass of champagne.*
Mi hermano me **pidió prestado** cinco dólares.	*My brother borrowed five dollars from me.*
Los chicos le **preguntaron** a su padre por qué el cielo es azul.	*The children asked their father why the sky is blue.*

Criar and crecer

The verb pair **criar** and **crecer** frequently cause confusion even for more advanced learners. This is partly because they sound so much alike, but more importantly because in various ways they involve the notions of growing: growing up, growing physically, and being cared for.

It may seem comical, but the following distinctions seem to help students avoid errors most of the time, even though they are not mutually exclusive differences. For children and animals, the verb to use is **criar**, which means *to raise*. If by *to grow up* you mean *to be raised*, you need **criar**, because *to grow up* doesn't focus on the physical maturing of a person.

Of course, children, animals, and plants also increase in stature, so in such cases, **crecer** is the verb to use. Related to **crecer**, particularly when speaking of plants (but also of a person's education), is the verb **cultivar**. It also is a friendly cognate.

Los padres de Juanito lo **criaron** bien, pues tiene buenos modales.	*Johnny's parents raised him well, he has such good manners.*
El maíz **crece** muy rápido en los calurosos meses del verano.	*Corn grows very quickly in the hot summer months.*
Los adolescentes parecen **crecer** ante los ojos.	*Teenagers seem to grow before your eyes.*
En Hawaii, se **cultivan** orquídeas exóticas.	*In Hawaii, they grow exotic orchids.*
Es importante descubrir y **cultivar** los talentos naturales.	*It is important to discover and cultivate your innate talents.*

Salir and dejar

The verb pair **salir** and **dejar** are often introduced with the primary meanings of *to leave* and *leave behind*. It is best, however, to translate **salir** as *to exit*. It is always followed by the preposition **de**, which helps recall its meaning as *to exit from*. Moreover, **dejar**, followed by an infinitive, means *to allow* (to do something). These two verbs also form an interesting constellation of uses, in part due to associated uses of the curious auxiliary verb **acabar de** + infinitive, which translates as *to have just*, and also to the uses of **dejar de** + infinitive which means *to quit* (doing something). Let's examine the various uses of these verbs.

Mi amigo **salió** del cuarto de baño.	*My friend came out of the restroom.*
Mi amigo **dejó** sus llaves en el cuarto de baño.	*My friend left his keys in the restroom.*
Los padres de mi amigo no lo **dejaron** ir a la fiesta de Juana.	*My friend's parents didn't let him go to Jane's party.*
Mi amigo **dejó** de fumar.	*My friend quit smoking.*
Mi amigo **acaba** de salir del cuarto de baño.	*My friend just came out of the restroom.*

Finally, just as we've seen how there is no simple Spanish verb for *to borrow*, there is no simple verb meaning *to drop*. The phrase **dejar caer** is used—literally, *to allow to fall*.

Cuando abrió la puerta, mi amiga **dejó caer** los libros.	*When my friend opened the door, she dropped the books.*

Mover(se) and mudarse

Finally, the verbs **mover(se)** and **mudarse** are often confused because **mover** is a false cognate when one refers to changing abodes. The verb **mover** means *to move*—but in the sense of moving an object, such as a pencil. In the reflexive, it means *to move about*, as in doing exercises or dancing.

The verb for changing one's residence is exclusively **mudarse**—and it is always reflexive in this usage. The verb **mudar** is often used with the preposition **de** when referring to changing one's clothes, opinions, and so forth. It is also the verb used to refer to a reptile *moulting* (changing skin) and even for when a child *changes* his or her baby teeth for permanent ones: **mudar los dientes**—and it is *not* reflexive when used in these latter senses.

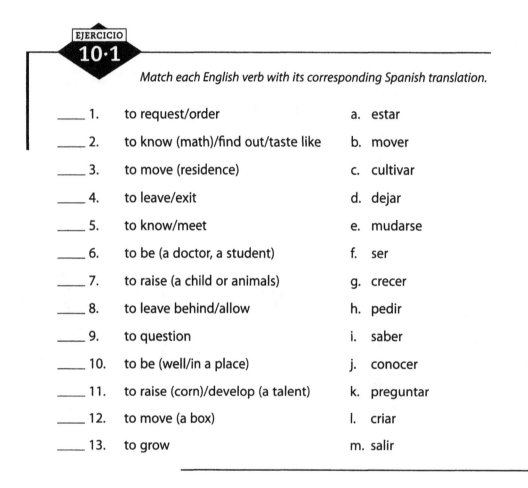

EJERCICIO
10·1

Match each English verb with its corresponding Spanish translation.

_____ 1.	to request/order	a.	estar
_____ 2.	to know (math)/find out/taste like	b.	mover
_____ 3.	to move (residence)	c.	cultivar
_____ 4.	to leave/exit	d.	dejar
_____ 5.	to know/meet	e.	mudarse
_____ 6.	to be (a doctor, a student)	f.	ser
_____ 7.	to raise (a child or animals)	g.	crecer
_____ 8.	to leave behind/allow	h.	pedir
_____ 9.	to question	i.	saber
_____ 10.	to be (well/in a place)	j.	conocer
_____ 11.	to raise (corn)/develop (a talent)	k.	preguntar
_____ 12.	to move (a box)	l.	criar
_____ 13.	to grow	m.	salir

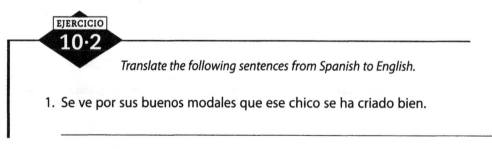

EJERCICIO
10·2

Translate the following sentences from Spanish to English.

1. Se ve por sus buenos modales que ese chico se ha criado bien.

_____

2. Mi amigo ruso sabe mucho de la física y la astronomía.

_____

3. Ese libro fue impreso en Barcelona.

———————————————————————————————————————

4. "Yo soy un hombre sincero, de donde crece la palma." (*José Martí*)

———————————————————————————————————————

5. Se me ha roto la caña de pescar.

———————————————————————————————————————

6. ¿Dónde y cuándo se conocieron sus padres?

———————————————————————————————————————

7. Las papas fritas se frieron hace unos minutos.

———————————————————————————————————————

8. El centro comercial no está precisamente en el centro de la ciudad.

———————————————————————————————————————

9. Los coches han sido fabricados con mucho cuidado.

———————————————————————————————————————

10. Yo conocía bien a Adele en la secundaria pero luego perdimos el contacto.

———————————————————————————————————————

11. En este momento, estoy sentado ante la computadora, escribiendo esto.

———————————————————————————————————————

12. Ya tengo la carta escrita para el jefe.

———————————————————————————————————————

13. En México, se ha cultivado el maíz desde hace miles de años.

———————————————————————————————————————

14. El gato no se movió de su sitio en dos horas, ya que esperaba que saliera el ratón.

———————————————————————————————————————

15. ¿Estás bien, chico? Te ves preocupado.

———————————————————————————————————————

16. Mi hija tenía tres años cuando nos mudamos a Seattle.

———————————————————————————————————————

17. La fiesta fue en casa de Julieta y fue fantástica.

———————————————————————————————————————

18. El niño todavía no se había puesto la chaqueta cuando salió para la escuela.

———————————————————————————————————————

19. Ayúdame a mover el sofá, por favor.

_____

20. La tienda estará abierta hasta a eso de las nueve.

_____

EJERCICIO
10·3

Translate the following sentences from English to Spanish.

1. We left our car at home.

_____

2. The bird was covered with tar.

_____

3. Said and done.

_____

4. He was married but his sister has always been single.

_____

5. Her parents won't let her watch TV. (_don't_ use **permitir**)

_____

6. Do you know Mary well?

_____

7. They will be sleeping for a couple of hours.

_____

8. He's boring.

_____

9. José is Mexican.

_____

10. This is a silk dress.

_____

11. The party is on the beach.

_____

12. When he left, he did not leave his memories.

_____

13. This is my father's car.

_____

14. He knew the lyrics to dozens of songs.

_____

15. Are you tired? (**Uds.**) (*don't* use **sueño**)

_____

16. Julius Caesar is dead.

_____

17. We met in 1990.

_____

18. She has returned the book.

_____

19. The confessed criminal has told the truth.

_____

20. You have just finished this exercise. (**tú**)

_____

Using verbs to show politeness

I'm sure you've learned to say **por favor**. This expression is generally sufficient to show courtesy to your listener, but it isn't the only means to indicate various degrees of earnestness when making a request. Compared with Spanish, English is relatively poor in terms of verbs or phrases for expressing politeness without seeming sarcastic. The word *please* is pretty much all that English speakers have at hand to verbally express politeness without adding verbiage that makes the speaker seem "over the top."

The use of **deber, querer,** and **poder** as helping verbs is progressively more polite in the present, conditional, and imperfect subjunctive. While they convey no difference in meaning, they display a great difference in tone for indicating three degrees, or gradations, of politeness in Spanish. In other words, the increasing gradations of politeness are shown by means of the tenses and moods used. Learning the forms in this chapter will place you beyond the bare territory of **por favor** and show that you are more socially functional than those who cannot manage these forms properly.

Like all helping verbs, these three verbs are used to introduce an infinitive (without any preposition between them). It is worth noticing that they have to do with the three aspects of the human mind: **poder** shows ability, capacity, or power (*can, could*): **querer** expresses volition or the will (*want* or *desire*); and **deber** indicates a moral obligation (*ought, should,* and *owe*).

Other auxiliary verbs or verb phrases that indicate moral obligation or necessity cannot be used as **deber** is to express degrees of politeness. The moral obligation expressed by **deber** is not as strong as that conveyed by **tener que** + infinitive, **necesitar** + infinitive, or the impersonal **hay que** + infinitive. Thus, unlike what many dictionaries indicate, **deber** is not the best translation for *must*, when *must* really means business.

Tenemos que pagar los impuestos cada año.	*We have to pay taxes every year.*
Necesitan ponerse loción o se van a quemar.	*They need to put on lotion or they will get a sunburn.*
Deben escribir una carta a su abuela.	*They should write a letter to their grandmother.*

In the present tense, **deber, querer,** and **poder** create unadorned statements and questions. They are neither polite nor impolite (of course, spoken tone could incline them either way). Consider the following examples:

Alejandra, **debes** practicar la flauta si quieres tocar en la sinfonía.	*Alexandra, you should practice the flute if you want to play in the symphony.*
¿**Puedes** acompañarme a la playa este fin de semana?	*Can you go to the beach with me this weekend?*
¿**Quieres** preparar la cena esta noche?	*Do you want to fix dinner tonight?*

When the verb tenses or moods in these same examples are changed to the conditional (technically a mood, not a tense), the statements and questions become more polite:

Alejandra, **deberías** practicar la flauta si quieres tocar en la sinfonía.	*Alexandra, you ought to practice the flute if you want to play in the symphony.*
¿**Podrías** acompañarme a la playa este fin de semana?	*Could you go to the beach with me this weekend?*
¿**Querrías** preparar la cena esta noche?	*Would you like to fix dinner tonight?*

The English language is incapable of adequately expressing just how much more polite these statements and questions become when the helping verb is in the imperfect subjunctive because any attempt to reflect this gradation would sound obsequious or even sarcastic. It isn't that English speakers can't be as polite, it is because our tonal and verbal arsenals are different from those of Spanish. Nevertheless, in the following examples, I have tried to approximate this degree of politeness by augmenting them with an intensifying adverb or some other expression.

Alejandra, **debieras** practicar la flauta si quieres tocar en la sinfonía.	*Alexandra, you really ought to practice the flute if you want to play in the symphony.*
¿**Pudieras** acompañarme a la playa este fin de semana?	*Could you, would you please, go to the beach with me this weekend?*
¿**Quisieras** preparar la cena esta noche?	*Would you mind fixing dinner tonight, please?*

Since the conditional form of **querer** (**querrías** in the example sounds so close to the imperfect forms of this verb (**quería**, **querías**), even native speakers of Spanish tend to not use it, preferring to use the imperfect subjunctive—**quisiera**, **quisieras**—which is the most polite form. Why not? It never hurts to be civil.

Due to the difficulty of expressing this most polite degree in English, many Spanish speakers are mistakenly labeled as impolite or sarcastic by English speakers who are unaware of this feature of Spanish. Consider how the last question could come off if a Spanish speaker, who has not mastered the wide range of tones in spoken English, were to attempt embellishing English in an attempt to reflect the politeness of Spanish.

¿Quisieras preparar la cena esta noche?	*Would you* really *be so kind as to fix dinner tonight, please?*

It's a good lesson in cultural sensitivity at the most basic level—language—where culture is inextricably embedded.

Give the proper form of the three helping verbs for the given subject pronouns in the tense and mood indicated.

1. (deber) él/imperfect subjunctive _____

2. (poder) tú/present indicative _____

3. (querer) ella/conditional _____

4. (querer) nosotros/imperfect subjunctive _____

5. (poder) Ud./imperfect subjunctive _____

6. (deber) Uds./conditional _____

7. (poder) yo/conditional _____

8. (deber) tú/imperfect subjunctive _____

9. (poder) yo/present indicative _____

10. (deber) ella/conditional _____

11. (querer) Ud./present indicative _____

12. (querer) vosotros/conditional _____

Translate the following sentences from Spanish to English.

1. Juan no debería manejar tan rápido.

   _____

2. Por favor, ¿podría Ud. ayudarme con esta maleta?

   _____

3. Creo que ella quisiera salir con Juan.

   _____

4. Pues, deberías ir al baile.

   _____

5. ¿Pudieran esperar hasta que lleguemos?

   _____

6. Yo querría probar este postre.

   _____

7. ¿Puedes echar una mano a esta tarea?

_____

8. Es obvio—Ella debe dejar de fumar.

_____

9. Por mucho que quisiéramos prestarle el dinero, no tenemos tanto.

_____

10. ¿Quieres comprar la ensalada si yo compro la carne?

_____

11. Si de veras quieren aprender la lección, deberían apagar la tele.

_____

12. Es cierto que quiero hacer la tarea, pero no dispongo de tiempo ahora.

_____

13. Ellos quisieran contribuir más a la organización.

_____

14. Mis hermanos podrían ayudarte mañana.

_____

15. ¿Pudieras tener la bondad de pedirle que venga a la reunión?

_____

16. Juanito, no debieras dejar de asistir a las lecciones de música.

_____

17. Mis primas quieren manejar ahora.

_____

18. ¡Con mucho gusto pudiéramos respaldarle en la campaña!

_____

19. Yo sé lo que debo hacer; es cuestión de no perder el ánimo.

_____

20. ¿Pueden Uds. enviarnos las herramientas dentro de un par de días?

_____

Translate the following sentences from English to Spanish. For the sake of eliciting the various degrees of politeness, the word really *is used in regular type to show the middle degree of politeness. When* really *is italicized, it indicates the most polite degree. For the forms of* **poder**, could *indicates the middle degree of politeness and* really *or* kindly, *when used with* could *and italicized, indicate the most polite degree.*

1. I *really* would like to go with you, but I can't. (**tú**)

_____

2. She really ought to bring her friend.

_____

3. We ought to read more.

_____

4. Can you come help me fix dinner? (**tú**)

_____

5. His friends *really* could do more for him.

_____

6. They ought to have returned the correct key to me.

_____

7. We *really* want to go to the movies with you (**tú**).

_____

8. She wants to invite John to the party.

_____

9. They *really* would like to bring their dog.

_____

10. My sister really ought to practice the violin more.

_____

11. Could you *kindly* turn off the radio? (**Uds.**)

_____

12. She and Ana *really* ought to thank their mother.

_____

13. He would like to loan you the money if you can pay him soon. (**Ud.**)

_____

14. His friend really should stop smoking.

_____

15. Could you bring me the chair? (**tú**)

_____

16. Wouldn't you and your friends _really_ like to go to the beach?

_____

17. She would come, but she can't.

_____

18. He and I ought to fix the car.

_____

19. You really ought to go to school. (**Ud.**) (use **asistir a**)

_____

20. I _really_ would like to invite you to lunch. (**tú**)

_____

Translating *ago* with hacer clauses

12

If you look up the word *ago* in most bilingual dictionaries, you'll discover that Spanish has no one-word equivalent for it. English speakers make handy and concise use of it all the time. The word *ago* enables English speakers to refer to actions in the past, measuring backward from the present. Logically, both English and Spanish use a verb in the past tense to do this. But Spanish commonly uses a construction that baffles English speakers—until they learn to accept it as a whole. This chapter will teach you how to use the verb **hacer** to ask and answer more complex questions about the temporal relationship between events—putting them on a time line that is every bit as clear as English, and quite formulaic.

There is no English structure to guide English-speaking students of Spanish and enable them to grasp the ways Spanish routinely frames the temporal notions that the **hacer** time clauses refer to. Thus, it is important to know what these Spanish structures mean in English, and not merely what the individual words mean.

The verb **hacer** is used in three ways. While each one follows the same structure, the use of the tenses of **hacer** and another verb render different meanings. Each structure denotes distinct relationships between the moment of speaking and an event, events, or situations in the past.

Present perfect meaning

The first structure we will examine shows *how long* something has been going on relative to the moment of speaking. It shows how an action that began in the past is either still going on or whose influence or impact is still being felt. This should sound familiar if you have learned the present perfect in Spanish or know the verb tense this grammatical term refers to. The difficulty for English speakers is that when when one wishes to express *how long* something has been going on, the present perfect tense is rarely used in Spanish. Observe the following example and notice that the translation into English uses, as it must, the present perfect, but in Spanish the verb **hacer** is used.

> **Hace** una hora que **escribo** esta carta. *I have been writing this letter for an hour.*

Notice the structure: the present indicative, third-person singular form of the verb **hacer**, followed by a measure of time, then **que**, then the sentence finishing with another verb in the present. This structure shows what action began in the past and continues into the present and can be summarized as follows:

present indicative of **hacer** (third-person singular) +
measure of time + **que** + verb (present tense)

The sentence could also be structured like this:

Escribo esta carta **desde hace** una hora.   *I've been writing this letter since an hour ago/for an hour.*

Just as an English speaker would understand, so too the Spanish speaker grasps immediately that the person making this statement began writing a letter an hour ago and still is writing it.

How to express the concept of *ago*

An action that began in the past doesn't have to be going on still, in the literal sense, in order for its impact to be felt at the moment of speaking. Notice the following example, supposing the speaker is turning down an invitation to eat lunch. This is a sentence whose English translation requires *ago*:

Hace una hora que **comí.**   *I ate an hour ago.*

Notice that the structure of this sentence is identical to the first example. The verb **hacer** is still in the same form as before and is followed by a measure of time, then the conjunction **que**; but the verb that ends the thought is in the preterit.

present indicative of **hacer** (third-person singular) +
measure of time + **que** + verb (preterit tense)

It is this whole structure and the relationship of the tenses that combine to create the equivalent of the notion expressed by the English word *ago*. It could also be structured as follows:

Comí hace una hora.   *I ate an hour ago.*

Pluperfect in meaning

The third way **hacer** is used in a time clause expresses how long something *had been going on* but does not tell us how long ago the action was happening. As the following model shows, Spanish uses the imperfect indicative of the two verbs in the **hacer** time clause and a verb in the preterit outside the **hacer** time clause; its English translation requires a combination of the pluperfect and another in the past tense.

Hacía cinco meses que María **estudiaba**   *Mary had been studying French for five*
francés cuando decidió cambiar   *months when she decided to switch*
al español.   *to Spanish.*

Notice that the structure, up to the adverb **cuando,** is the same as in the previous examples. What is different is that both **hacer** and the verb completing the time-clause structure are in the imperfect indicative.

imperfect indicative of **hacer** (third-person singular) +
measure of time + **que** + verb (imperfect indicative tense)

This structure establishes the sequence of how, at some time in the past (we are not informed how long ago), Mary began studying French, continued for five months, then switched to Spanish—three neat facts strung on a verbal time line.

You may also encounter the following structure, which is useful for providing background information. Notice that it too translates as pluperfect and that, as in the previous example, we do not know how long ago John followed his routine.

Juan **hacía** ejercicios todos los miércoles **desde hacía** años.
Hacía años que Juan **hacía** ejercicios todos los miércoles.

John had been working out every Wednesday for years.

Asking questions

The **hacer** time clauses are also used to ask questions. Here are the two types of question structures that could have been asked to elicit the previous examples. The word **tiempo** is in parentheses to indicate that it is optional.

¿**Cuánto (tiempo) hace** que **escribes** la carta?
¿**Hace cuánto (tiempo)** que **escribes** la carta?

How long have you been writing the letter?

¿**Cuánto (tiempo) hace** que **comiste**?
¿**Hace cuánto (tiempo)** que **comiste**?

How long ago did you eat?

¿**Cuánto (tiempo) hacía** que María **estudiaba** francés cuando decidió cambiar al español?
¿**Hacía cuánto (tiempo)** que María **estudiaba** francés cuando decidió cambiar al español?

How long had Mary studied French when she decided to switch to Spanish?

Ways to say *I wonder*

It frequently happens that not long after Spanish learners have begun to take baby steps to converse with native Spanish speakers, they realize just how often the word *wonder* comes to mind and find themselves at a loss to express it. Consultations with bilingual dictionaries usually leave English speakers unsatisfied. As it turns out, there are five principal ways in which this word is used in English and, as it happens with phrasal verbs, so too do these various usages have as many solutions in Spanish. Since Spanish only has nouns (e.g., **maravilla, prodigio**), but no verbs for this word, the solutions do not involve any translation of *wonder* itself, but instead use ways to express what the English word intends.

The first usage of *wonder* is to express a *polite request*, such as:

Me gustaría si pudieras cenar conmigo.

I was wondering if you could have dinner with me. (Literally: It would please me if you could dine with me.)

This usage of *wonder* is accomplished in Spanish by the use of the conditional plus the imperfect subjunctive. There are other simpler solutions that do not involve the subjunctive—by avoiding a change of subject:

Me gustaría cenar contigo.

Literally: *It would please me to dine with you.*

The second use of *wonder* is to express *curiosity*. For instance, you may wonder if something has happened yet:

A **ver** si me ha llegado el cheque en el correo.

I wonder if my check has come in the mail. (Literally: Let's see if the check for me has arrived in the mail.)

Another solution for expressing this aspect of *wonder* is to employ the *future of probability*, a usage of the simple future tense in Spanish that defies translation into English:

¿Me **habrá** llegado el cheque?

Literally: *Will the check for me have arrived?*

The third way that English speakers use *wonder* is to suggest *mentally weighing* something, or turning something over in one's mind. A handy way to remember this usage is to note that the verbs both for *turning* and *to ask oneself* can be used in Spanish when this is what is meant in English.

Hacía varios días que yo **le daba muchas vueltas** a esto.

I had been wondering about this for a few days.

Me preguntaba si debería comprar ese auto.

I was wondering if I should buy that car. (Literally: I was asking myself if I should buy that car.)

The fourth way English uses *wonder* is to express *uncertainty*:

Ella **no sabía** si debiera solicitar ese trabajo.

She was wondering if she should apply for that job.

Finally, the fifth use of *wonder* is to show a *lack of surprise*:

No me extraña/sorprende que no me haya llamado—está todavía en el trabajo.

No wonder he didn't call me—he's still at work.

Con razón no me habías llamado, ¡estabas todavía en el trabajo!

No wonder you hadn't called me—you were still at work!

EJERCICIO

12·1

Select the translation that best reflects the meaning of the following sentences in English.

1. She has lived in Mexico for two years.

   a. Ella vivió en México por dos años.

   b. Ella ha vivido en México por dos años.

   c. Hace dos años que ella vive en México.

2. I wonder where my dog is.

   a. ¿Dónde está el perro?

   b. ¿Dónde está mi perro?

   c. ¿Dónde estará mi perro?

3. They had been in Buenos Aires for a week when they decided to buy a car.

   a. Estaban en Buenos Aires por una semana cuando decidieron comprar un auto.

   b. Habían estado en Buenos Aires por una semana y decidieron comprar un auto.

   c. Hacía una semana que estaban en Buenos Aires cuando decidieron comprar un auto.

4. I started cooking an hour ago.

   a. He cocinado por una hora.

   b. Empecé a cocinar hace una hora.

   c. Hace una hora que cocino.

5. How long has it been since you've been to the dentist?

   a. ¿Desde cuándo no has ido al dentista?

   b. ¿Cuánto tiempo hace que no has ido al dentista?

   c. ¿Cuándo fue la última vez que fuiste al dentista?

6. How many days were you lost in the woods?

   a. ¿Hace cuánto tiempo que te perdiste en el bosque?

   b. ¿Cuántos días hacía que andabas perdido en el bosque?

   c. ¿Por cuántos días estuviste perdido en el bosque?

7. We were wondering if you'd like to go shopping tomorrow.

   a. Queremos saber si quieres ir de compras mañana.

   b. Nos gustaría saber si quisieras ir de compras mañana.

   c. Nos dará gusto si quieres ir de compras mañana.

8. I was wondering if the package had arrived.

   a. Me preguntaba si el paquete había llegado.

   b. Me preguntó si el paquete había llegado.

   c. ¿Me habrá llegado el paquete?

9. No wonder he didn't run. He had a broken foot.

   a. No es una sorpresa que no corriera. Se le había roto el pie.

   b. No me sorprende que no corriera. Tenía una rotura del pie.

   c. Con razón no corrió. Se rompió el pie.

10. I was wondering if I should accept the job.

    a. Yo no sé si deba aceptar el puesto.

    b. Yo no sabía si debía aceptar el puesto.

    c. Me pregunto si es un puesto bueno para mí.

11. They opened the store two hours ago.

    a. Hacía dos horas que habían abierto la tienda.

    b. Ellos abren la tienda a las dos.

    c. Hace dos horas que abrieron la tienda.

12. He and I had been friends for years when he moved away.

    a. Él y yo somos amigos desde hace años, pero se mudó hace tiempo.

    b. Cuando él se mudó, hacía años que él y yo éramos amigos.

    c. Él se mudó cuando hacía años que éramos amigos.

13. Arnold had been driving the bus for an hour when he got sick.

    a. Arnold se enfermó después de manejar el autobús por una hora.

    b. Hacía una hora que Arnold manejaba el autobús cuando se enfermó.

    c. Arnold estuvo enfermo por una hora después de manejar el autobús.

14. John was working at the newspaper for years.

    a. Juan trabajaba para el periódico desde hacía años.

    b. Juan ha trabajado para el periódico por muchos años.

    c. Juan estuvo trabajando para el periódico por años y años.

15. How long had you (**tú**) been sleeping when I called?

    a. ¿Cuántas horas habías dormido cuando yo te llamé?

    b. ¿Por cuánto tiempo dormiste antes de que te llamara?

    c. ¿Hacía cuánto tiempo que dormías cuando te llamé?

16. When she met her boyfriend, she had been traveling in Europe for a month.

    a. Conoce a su novio desde cuando estuvo viajando por Europa por un mes.

    b. Cuando conoció a su novio, hacía un mes que viajaba por Europa.

    c. Ella viajaba por Europa por un mes cuando conoció a su novio.

17. I wonder what will happen tomorrow.

    a. ¿Qué pasa mañana?

    b. ¿Qué pasó esta mañana?

    c. Me pregunto qué pasará mañana.

18. No wonder he gained weight—all he has been eating for weeks is pizza.

    a. No me sorprende que esté más gordo—lo único que ha comido en semanas es pizza.

    b. Con razón aumentó de peso—hace semanas que no come sino pizza.

    c. Gran cosa que se está engordando—no come nada excepto pizza.

19. When he left work, Arnold had been on the phone for an hour.

    a. Cuando salió del trabajo, hacía una hora que Arnold hablaba por teléfono.

    b. Arnold habló por una hora en el teléfono y luego salió del trabajo.

    c. Arnold salió del trabajo e hizo una llamada por teléfono.

20. They lived in Mazatlán three years ago.

    a. Hacía tres años que vivían en Mazatlán.

    b. Hace tres años que vivieron en Mazatlán.

    c. Vivieron en Mazatlán por tres años.

EJERCICIO
12·2

*Recompose these dehydrated sentences about **hacer** time clauses, ways to express wonder, and probability in the present and the past. Watch for when you'll need to add articles, nouns, prepositions—and **que**.*

1. tú/preguntarse/qué nota/sacar/en último examen.

   _____

2. ahora/hacer/dos horas/ellos/correr/en el parque.

   _____

3. hacer/dos años/él/jugar al fútbol/cuando/romperse la pierna.

   _____

4. ayer/a las tres/yo/estar/en la biblioteca/,¿dónde/estar/Juan?

   _____

5. ¿cuántos/años/hacer/tú/conocer/tu novia/cuando/casarse?

_____

6. hacer/una hora/yo/comer

_____

7. no te sorprende/María y Juan/casarse

_____

8. le gustar (a él)/si/ellos/acompañarle/cine

_____

9. ayer/ellos/esperar/tú/llegar/pero (tú) no/llegar/¿dónde/estar (tú)?

_____

10. ¿quién/saber/dónde/estar/llaves/ahora/? Él/perder (llaves)/todo/tiempo.

_____
_____

EJERCICIO
12·3

Translate the following sentences from Spanish to English.

1. Nos mudamos a este pueblo hace un par de años, cuando mi hija tenía tres años.

_____

2. No le sorprendió que su hermano ganara la carrera, ya que hacía un año que se entrenaba.

_____

3. A ver si no hay un cheque en mi buzón.

_____

4. Con razón ha sido detenido el Sr. Acero—hace años que defrauda a los empleados.

_____

5. Juan se preguntaba por qué hacía tiempo que María no le contestaba cuando la llamaba.

_____

6. Mis padres vivían allí desde hacía años.

_____

7. ¿Cuánto hace que no ves a tus padres?

_____

8. Hice muchos ejercicios hace una hora.

_____

9. ¿Cuánto hacía que Teresa ponía la mesa? Me pregunto si no se distrae mucho.

_____

10. Nos gustaría si tuvieras la bondad de devolvernos el libro que te prestamos hace una semana.

_____

11. ¿Hace cuánto que el sastre te arregló el abrigo?

_____

12. Hacía tiempo que el mecánico se tardaba en inspeccionar el auto.

_____

13. Cuando detuvieron al Sr. Acero, hacía meses que lo vigilaban las autoridades.

_____

14. Cinco de mis amigos y yo fuimos testigos de un evento paranormal hace tres semanas.

_____

15. Duró sólo un minuto o menos, pero nos pareció que hacía una hora que lo veíamos.

_____

16. Hacía una hora que ensayábamos cuando Jorge hizo que se apagara la luz.

_____

17. ¿Mi amigo le habrá dejado un mensaje de voz a Juan?

_____

18. Cuando se les rompió la ventana hace un mes, ellos no sabían si debían llamar a la policía.

_____

19. A ver si mi padre no me haya llamado.

_____

20. Me pregunto qué me hubiera sucedido si no me hubiera casado con ella.

_____

*Translate the following sentences from English to Spanish. Use **hacer** time clauses when dealing with time frames, not perfect or pluperfect tenses.*

1. Who knows how he got that job a year ago.

   _____

2. She wondered whether he would call her or not.

   _____

3. They had worked for an hour when the boss came in.

   _____

4. Mr. Acero hadn't told the truth for years.

   _____

5. When the play ended, she realized that she had been sleeping for twenty minutes.

   _____

6. He had been trying to borrow money from his brother for a month.

   _____

7. We have been the owners of the business for a year.

   _____

8. The flowers dried up because she had not watered them for a week.

   _____

9. The dog has been sleeping for three hours.

   _____

10. I had lived in Mazatlán for four years when I decided to return to the USA.

    _____

11. The bread had been baking for twenty minutes when the power went out.

    _____

12. Her cousin went to Europe for two weeks about six months ago.

    _____

13. How many years ago was your grandfather born?

    _____

14. How long had you been shopping when you realized that you had lost your credit card? (**tú**)

    _____

15. The clothes had been hanging out to dry for only ten minutes when it started to rain.

    _____

16. She's been in her room studying for two hours.

    _____

17. When the submarine surfaced, it had been under the polar ice cap for over two months.

    _____

18. He has been snoring in the rocking chair for a least an hour.

    _____

19. We woke him up after he had slept for two hours.

    _____

20. No wonder you're tired: these sentences are hard! (**tú**)

    _____

The **gustar** verb family

13

There is no Spanish verb that corresponds to the English verb *to like*. This should not cause as many problems as it seems to. In this chapter, you'll discover a few tricks that will dispel any confusion you might have about the verb **gustar** and other verbs of the **gustar** family.

Gustar

Textbooks try to get students to use this verb correctly by resorting to a bit of subterfuge: they introduce it in a preliminary lesson, including it in some short, model dialogues, using questions such as **¿Te gusta...?** and a reply of **Sí, me gusta...** or **No, no me gusta...** to condition students to use the verb correctly. It seems like a good idea to introduce this structure of indirect object + **gustar** in the third-person singular as if it were a vocabulary item to be learned whole. Unfortunately, the translations of **gustar** in the dialogues often are *Do you like . . .* and *Yes, I do like . . .* or *No, I don't like. . . .* These translations soon cause confusion when students learn to conjugate verbs and discover that the first-person singular (in the present indicative) ends in **-o** and not in **-a**. Later, when students encounter the lesson about **gustar** and the **gustar** family of verbs, usually in conjunction with indirect object pronouns, confusion about the one often is compounded by confusion about the other.

Another problem in learning how to use the verb **gustar** is that when students move on to intermediate or advanced study, they discover that **gustar** can be used in more than just the third-person singular and plural. The earlier problems resurface at this point for some students because they were improperly conditioned. If you have experienced these sorts of confusions, then this chapter will resolve them.

Let's start with English, but not with the verb *to like* (since we know it is the source of the problem). The English verb *disgust* works grammatically just like the Spanish verb **gustar**. Happily, too, its root is quite obviously from the same Latin root as the Spanish verb. The English verb *disgust* expresses a stronger emotion than the Spanish verb **disgustar**, but let's examine the following example:

    Me disgustan las anchoas.   *Anchovies disgust me. (More accurately: Anchovies displease me).*

From this sentence, we need only make a short hop in order to see how the verb **gustar** really works—and how its meaning requires it to work as it does! For the sake of example, recognize that *dis-* negates the verb it is prefixed to, and let's remove it and pretend for a moment that English has a verb *gust*, which means the opposite of *disgust*. In the following example, note that although the word orders

111

of English and Spanish are different, the grammatical relationships between subject (**anchoas**/*anchovies*), object (**me**/*me*) and verb (**gusta**/*gust*) in both languages are the same.

Me gustan las anchoas.   *Anchovies gust me.*

The verb **gustar**, in a way, makes more sense than *to like*. Consider this: although an English speaker says *I like pizza*, the only thing the subject does is *eat* the pizza. It's the pizza that does the *pleasing*.

Doler

The verb **doler** causes similar confusion because, just as **gustar** means *to please* instead of *to like*, **doler** means *to be painful* instead of *to hurt*. However, having seen the grammatical relationship by some creative manipulation of the verb *disgust*, the following examples reveal how its meaning requires it to be used in the same way:

Me duelen los pies.   *My feet hurt (me).*
A Juan **le duele** una muela.   *John's molar hurts (him).*

Other members of the **gustar** family

The English counterparts of the rest of the verbs in the **gustar** family work grammatically in English in the same way as they do in Spanish. Examine the following sentences using **fascinar**, **encantar**, and **interesar**. Note that the second English translation in each example is the most common way English speakers express these ideas—and the reason why they often have difficulty using the Spanish verbs correctly: Spanish prefers verbs in the active voice to express these ideas whereas English prefers adjectives and passive constructions.

Nos fascinan historias sobre extraterrestres.

Stories about extraterrestrials fascinate us.
We are fascinated by stories about extraterrestrials.

Les encanta escuchar óperas.

Listening to operas enchants them.
They're enchanted by the opera. Or: *They just love operas.*

¿Te interesan las películas de espionaje?

Do spy movies interest you?
Are you interested in spy movies?

As an example of how **gustar** can be used in forms other than the third person, consider this short and amusing dialogue between two young people who have just started dating. She is a native speaker of Spanish; he is an English speaker who doesn't know that **gustar** can be in the first- or second-person forms.

In his first reply, he simply mumbles her question aloud, trying to figure it out. She, of course, understands it perfectly! Remember: **gustar** means *to please*; it does not mean *to like*.

Juana:	**¿Te gusto?**	*Do you like me?* (Literally: *Do I please you?*)
John:	**¿Te gusto?**	*Do you like me?* [puzzled: talking to himself]
Juana:	¡Claro que **me gustas**, pero quiero saber si yo te gusto a ti.	*Of course I like you, but I want to know if you like me.*
John:	Sí.	*Yes.*

Translate the following sentences from Spanish to English.

1. Me fascina la geometría pero no me gusta estudiar estadísticas.

_____

2. A mis padres, no les gustaba nada que yo hiciera travesuras en la escuela.

_____

3. ¿Qué te parece si vamos a Cancún de vacaciones?

_____

4. Esta mañana, me dolía la cabeza hasta que tomé una aspirina.

_____

5. Cuando la conocí, les conté a mis amigos en seguida cómo ella me encantaba.

_____

6. ¿Te interesa estudiar conmigo?

_____

7. A ese chico no le importó que su hermana no se sintiera bien.

_____

8. Espero que estos ejercicios les gusten a mis lectores.

_____

9. Juana tenía dolor de cabeza pero no le dolía el estómago.

_____

10. Yo sé que si fueras a España, te encantarían las tapas.

_____

11. De niño, le fascinaba observar a los insectos.

_____

12. Ese Sr. Acero no me ha caído bien nunca.

_____

13. Le pareció raro que a la niña no le gustara nada en la escuela.

_____

14. Antes, me interesaba la literatura, pero ahora me llaman más la atención la historia y las biografías.

_____

15. Al joven, yo le impresiono con lo que sé sobre la historia local.

_____

16. ¿No te importa nada la política? Pues, tal vez porque no les importamos mucho a los políticos.

_____

17. María, yo sé que le gustas a Enrique.

_____

18. Las plantas carnívoras le fascinan a mi amiga.

_____

19. ¿No te repugna el olor del humo de tabaco?

_____

20. Me duelen los oídos cuando oigo cantar a esa mujer.

_____

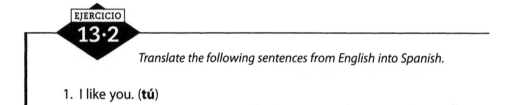

EJERCICIO
13·2

Translate the following sentences from English into Spanish.

1. I like you. (**tú**)

_____

2. Does she like me?

_____

3. Are you fascinated by classical music? (**vosotros**)

_____

4. Doesn't the way he writes seem strange to you? (**tú**)

_____

5. I think you like me. (**tú**)

_____

6. They used to be interested in playing chess, but not anymore.

_____

7. After she quit smoking, she gained weight.

_____

8. They don't like them (e.g., apples).

_____

9. Aren't you repulsed by violent movies? (**Uds.**)

_____

10. Money and power seemed to not matter to him after he returned from the war.

_____

11. We really like making ice cream.

_____

12. He was charmed by her smile.

_____

13. You don't impress me, Mr. Acero. (**tú**)

_____

14. My foot hurts.

_____

15. What most matters to you in life, Alexandra? (**tú**)

_____

16. Her mother's hands were hurting.

_____

17. It seemed strange to him that you liked asparagus. (**tú**)

_____

18. I hope you'll still be interested in studying Spanish after you finish this chapter! (**Uds.**)

_____

19. I'll be interested in the news.

_____

20. She likes me!

_____

Comparisons

Before you can compare any two (or more) people, things, or ideas, you have to be able to describe them. Doing that, as you know, requires knowledge of adjectives.

The positive degree

When an adjective is used to describe one person, thing, or idea, it is said to be in the *positive degree*. *Positive*, in this case, is simply a grammatical term and includes both good and bad qualities. The following three examples are simple statements in which the predicate adjectives attribute some quality—good, neutral, and bad, respectively.

Roberto es **alto**.	*Robert is tall.*
Esta manzana es **roja**.	*This apple is red.*
El Sr. Acero es **mentiroso**.	*Mr. Acero is a liar.*

These examples are clearly not comparisons. Another person or thing needs to be introduced for comparison with these subjects with respect to the different qualities.

The comparative degree

A comparison of two (or more) people, things, or ideas, whether they are equal or unequal comparisons, is called the *comparative degree*. The structure of a comparative sentence is very much like a mathematical equation: $X > Y$ (X is *greater* [than] Y) in which the word *than* is expressed by the conjunction **que**. The word **menos** can also be used, in which case it means $X < Y$ (X is *less* [than] Y). This mathematical abstraction suggests that the structure of unequal comparisons in English and Spanish is very similar.

Roberto es **más alto** que Enrique.	*Robert is taller than Henry.*
Esta manzana es **más roja** que la otra.	*The apple is redder than the other one.*
El Sr. Acero es **más mentiroso** que el diablo.	*Mr. Acero is a bigger liar than the devil.*
Hay **menos tráfico** en Acapulco que en Guadalajara.	*There is less traffic in Acapulco than in Guadalajara.*

Comparisons can be made with respect to *nouns*, *adjectives*, or *adverbs*, whether of equality or inequality. This can be seen in the following examples of comparisons of inequality.

Tengo **más libros** que ella.	*I have more books than she.*
Ella es **menos talentosa** que sus colegas.	*She is less talented than her colleagues.*
Él corre **más rápido** que yo.	*He runs faster than I.*

There are several adjectives in Spanish whose comparative forms are, or may be, irregular, depending on their meaning. Note that **más bueno** and **más malo** are used when speaking of character, as in the examples below.

POSITIVE DEGREE	COMPARATIVE DEGREE
bueno	más bueno *or* mejor
grande	más grande *or* mayor
joven	más joven *or* menor
malo	más malo *or* peor
mucho	más
pequeño	más pequeño *or* menor
poco	menos
viejo	más viejo *or* mayor

The forms **mejor** and **peor** are used when they refer to any quality other than moral ones, such as skills, talents, or other abilities. Likewise, **más grande** and **más pequeño** can refer to size or age, while **más joven** refers to age only. The form **menor** performs double duty, meaning either *younger* (particularly when referring to people) or *smaller* (referring to people or things). The comparative **más viejo** can be applied to people or things, while **mayor** refers always to age and mostly is used when comparing people's ages, such as siblings.

Yo soy **mayor** que mi prima.	*I am older than my cousin.*
La hermana de Jorge es **menor** que él.	*George's sister is younger than he.*

There are also two common adverbs that are used for description: **bien** (*well*) and **mal** (*badly* or *poorly*). Their comparative forms are the same as the irregular forms for **bueno** and **malo**— **mejor** and **peor**, respectively. The identical forms may lead a few learners to incorrectly use **bueno**, in particular, as an adverb.

Juan escribe **bien**.	*John writes well. (positive degree)*
Miguel escribe **mejor** que Juan.	*Michael writes better than John. (comparative degree)*
Mi hermano es **más grande** que yo.	*My brother is bigger than I am.*

In this last example, **más grande** also could mean *older*, unless clarified. Regional preferences exist with regard to the choice of **mayor/más grande** and **menor/más pequeño**.

Yo soy **mayor** que mi hermano.	*I am older than my brother.*

If these two statements are combined, any ambiguity of the first example is eliminated:

Mi hermano es **más grande** que yo, pero soy **mayor** que él.	*My brother is bigger than I am, but I'm older than he.*

The sentence structure for comparisons of equality is also similar in English and Spanish. Once again, comparisons are made with respect to nouns, adjectives, and adverbs. Note that when the comparison involves adjectives or adverbs, **tan** is used. The singular form **tanto (tanta)**, which means *as much*, is used with what are called non-count nouns—things that are not being or cannot be counted. The plurals—**tantos** and **tantas**—mean *as many*, and are used with things that are or can be counted. Consider the following examples:

Mis padres tienen **tanto dinero** como mis tíos.	*My parents have as much money as my uncle and aunt. (money is not being counted)*
Yo tengo **tantos dólares** como tú.	*I have as many dollars as you. (money is being, or could be counted)*
Elena es **tan guapa** como su hermana.	*Ellen is as pretty as her sister.*
Ella no juega al baloncesto **tan bien** como su hermano.	*She doesn't play basketball as well as her brother.*

The superlative degree

The third degree of comparison is called the *superlative degree*. It is used when there are at least three people, things, or ideas being compared and one among them stands out with respect to some quality. Three things should be noted in the following examples. First, the definite article is used before the words **más** and **menos** in order to set apart the person(s), thing(s), or idea(s) that stand out among the members of a group being compared with one another. Second, the preposition **de** is used where English uses *in* or *on*. Third, the irregular forms of the adjectives of the comparative degree are used in the superlative.

Tomás es **el más alto** de la clase.	*Thomas is the tallest in the class.*
Juana es **la más lista** de la familia.	*Jane is the smartest in the family.*
Miguel y Pablo son **los peores jugadores** del equipo.	*Michael and Paul are the worst players on the team.*
Mi hija es **la mejor cantante** del coro.	*My daughter is the best singer in the chorus.*

The absolute superlative

Spanish also has what is known as the absolute superlative. It is a one-word adjective form, built from the adjective of the positive degree by appending -**ísimo**, -**ísima**, -**ísimos**, or -**ísimas**. Although it existed in Latin, Spanish did not use it until the late 15th century when Italian poetry took the poetic world by storm and Spanish poets began incorporating many forms and styles from Italy. Because of pop culture, this form is probably familiar to most English speakers whether they have studied Spanish or not. It does not have a precise English translation and so the same idea is often conveyed with tone or hyperbolic (exaggerated) language. It is used when a person, thing, or idea is so beyond compare that mentioning any other person, thing, or idea with similar qualities would seem fruitless.

Goliat fue **altísimo**.	*Goliath was tall.*
La modelo de París fue **bellísima**.	*The Parisian model was drop-dead gorgeous.*
Algunas mujeres creen que Paul Newman fue **guapísimo**.	*Some women think that Paul Newman was a real hunk.*

When an indefinite pronoun is used to conclude a comparative construction, the negative form of the indefinite is used. In English, the positive form is used.

Ese hombre es **más corrupto que** nadie.	*That man is more corrupt than anyone.*
Más que nada me encanta cocinar.	*More than anything, I love to cook.*

Más and menos with numbers

To conclude this chapter on comparatives, let's examine the use of **más** and **menos** with numbers. The standard rule that most texts give is to use **de** in comparisons with numbers. Some texts comment on the use of **que** in comparisons involving numbers when the statement is negative. The best way to clear the air on this issue is to offer examples presenting all the possible combinations.

Más

Hay **más de** cinco libros en la mesa.	*There are more than five books on the table.*
No hay **más de** cinco libros en la mesa.	*There are no more than five books on the table. (there could be fewer, but five is the max)*
No hay **más que** cinco libros en la mesa.	*There are but five books on the table. (not four, not six, but exactly five)*

Menos

Hay **menos de** cinco libros en la mesa.	*There are fewer than five books on the table.*
No hay **menos de** cinco libros en la mesa.	*There are no fewer than five books on the table. (five is the minimum)*

Note: It is incorrect to use **menos que** with *numbers*, whether in an affirmative or negative sentence.

EJERCICIO
14·1

Recompose these dehydrated sentences. Using the elements given, create comparative sentences. You will have to supply missing words and conjugate the verbs correctly. You will also have to supply some verbs!

1. Tú/más alto/Tomás.

_____

2. Mi hermano/correr/tan/rápido/ellos.

_____

3. Su hermana/tener/dinero/como yo.

_____

4. Hoy/hacer/menos/frío/ayer.

_____

5. Llover/más/aquí/en Arizona.

_____

6. El Sr. Acero/tan malo/diablo.

_____

7. Juana/alumna/más lista/clase.

_____

8. Haber/menos/cinco libros/mesa.

_____

9. ¡Padres/siempre/mayores/sus hijos!

_____

10. Pedro/químico/más preparado/equipo.

_____

11. María y Teresa/bailar/mejor/yo.

_____

12. Estos dos/peores platos/menú.

_____

13. Me gusta/postre/más/el otro.

_____

14. ¡jugador/baloncesto/altísimo!

_____

15. Juanito/tener/tantos/juguetes/su hermanita.

_____

16. Haber/menos nieve/esta montaña/la otra.

_____

17. Carro/más costoso/otro.

_____

18. Ella/leer/revistas/como yo.

_____

19. Esa muchacha/más/interesante/de todas.

_____

20. La oveja/no beber/tanta agua/como el camello.

_____

Translate the following sentences from Spanish to English.

1. Los chicos no durmieron tantas horas como yo.

_____

2. Mi novia tiene el cabello tan largo como su mamá.

_____

3. Esa chica es guapísima.

_____

4. ¿Eres tan popular como él?

_____

5. ¿Tienes tantos amigos como yo?

_____

6. No creo que Juan sea menor que tú.

_____

7. ¿Cómo se llama el mayor de tus hermanos?

_____

8. No hay más que cinco jugadores en un equipo de baloncesto.

_____

9. Ella es tan llorona como su tía.

_____

10. ¿Cuál es el país más grande del mundo?

_____

11. Puerto Rico es menos grande que Cuba.

_____

12. Nueva York no tiene tantos habitantes como México, D.F.

_____

13. Hay menos de cuatro pizzas en el refrigerador.

_____

14. Eres tan amable como me dijeron.

_____

15. A Jorge le gusta jugar al tenis tanto como mirar películas.

_____

16. A mí me encanta nadar en el mar más que en los lagos.

_____

17. Estos dos son los más atléticos del grupo.

_____

18. Ella no tiene tanta energía como esperábamos.

_____

19. En la mesa hay tantos bolígrafos como lápices.

_____

20. Más que nada, le interesaba fabricar pescaditos de oro.

_____

Translate the following sentences from English to Spanish.

1. Who is the most important person in your life? (**tú**)

_____

2. What do your friends like to do more than anything else? (**Ud.**)

_____

3. She is the richest woman in the world.

_____

4. Do you have as many shirts as you have socks? (**Uds.**)

_____

5. She is the best swimmer on the team.

_____

6. She paints as much as he does.

_____

7. There are no fewer than one thousand books in this collection.

_____

8. Her mother sells more than I do.

_____

9. Which lake in the United States is the deepest?

_____

10. The Atlantic is smaller than the Pacific.

_____

11. His brother is younger than you. (**tú**)

_____

12. We are not the tallest players on the team.

_____

13. This watch costs as much as that one.

_____

14. Who has as many shoes as she?

_____

15. We are the best chefs in town.

_____

16. Venus can shine as brightly as an airplane's light.

_____

17. There are more fish in this lake than in that one.

_____

18. He is the worst chess player in the school.

_____

19. He goes to the movies as often as I do.

_____

20. She writes as well as she sings.

_____

Indefinite words

The Spanish language employs a small but sometimes bewildering array of indefinite words that, depending on their relationships to other words in a sentence, can function as pronouns or adjectives. Their affirmative forms usually pose few problems, but English speakers sometimes forget their corresponding negative forms—which *must* be used in negative constructions. Let's start with a list of high frequency words.

AFFIRMATIVE		NEGATIVE	
algo	*something*	nada	*nothing*
alguien	*someone*	nadie	*no one/nobody*
alguno	*some . . .*	ninguno	*none/not one . . .*

Of these words, **algo** and **nada** cannot refer to people, but **alguien** and **nadie** can only refer to people. In terms of usage, **alguien** is somewhat vaguer than **alguno**. Consider the following examples, noting that the subjunctive must be used in clauses that modify a non-existent person or thing:

Hay **algo** aquí que me parece raro.	*There is something here that seems strange to me.*
No hay **nada** en la mesa.	*There is nothing on the table.*
No hay **nada** en ese libro que pueda explicar la historia.	*There is nothing in that book that can explain history.*
Creo que hay **alguien** esperándome afuera.	*I think there is someone waiting for me outside.*
No hay **nadie** en la sala.	*There is no one in the room.*
No hay **nadie** que sepa tanto sobre esto como él.	*There is no one who knows so much about this as he does.*

In comparisons, **nadie** is used where English retains the affirmative form *anyone* or *anybody*:

En la cena, Juan comió más que **nadie**.	*At the dinner, John ate more than anyone.*

The words **alguno** and **ninguno** can serve either as adjectives or pronouns. When they are adjectives and precede a masculine noun, they drop the final -**o**, since they refer to an unspecified person, thing, or abstraction. When used to refer to a substance or an abstraction, they refer to an imprecise quantity, but not a large one. Let's consider their use as adjectives first:

Algún muchacho llamó hace una hora.	*Some guy called an hour ago.*

125

Lo que hace falta en la política es **alguna** más **honestidad**.	*What's missing in politics is a bit more honesty.*
Lucinda trajo **algún libro** ayer y no sé dónde está ahora.	*Lucinda brought some book yesterday and I don't know where it is now.*
Tengo **algunas revistas** en la mochila.	*I have some magazines in my backpack.*

The Spanish equivalent of the common English expression *some/one or another* is either **alguno que otro** or **algún que otro**; note that the feminine is not used because the masculine is the default gender for indefiniteness. Another more frequently encountered option in Spanish is to use the pronoun **cualquiera**, which is treated later in this chapter.

Si usted necesita ayuda, **alguno que otro** allí le puede atender.	*If you need help, anybody there can assist you.*

It may seem odd, but when **alguno** (in all its forms) is placed at the end of a clause, it is decidedly negative in meaning, similar to the English uses of *a single . . .* or *at all*. Observe the following examples, noting that the last one is somewhat more literary than conversational:

Juan no lo encontró en **parte alguna**.	*John didn't find it anywhere.*
No veo **barco alguno**.	*I don't see a single ship.*

Conversationally, this last example would be:

No veo **ningún barco**.	*I don't see a single ship.*

Spanish also has indefinite adverbs. Their affirmative forms have corresponding negative forms that must be used in negative constructions. The form **jamás** is stronger in tone than **nunca**.

AFFIRMATIVE		NEGATIVE	
también	*also, too*	tampoco	*(not) either* or *neither*
siempre	*always*	nunca, jamás	*never*

Me encanta *La boda de Fígaro*—¡ah!, y *La flauta mágica* **también**.	*I love* The Marriage of Figaro—*Oh! And* The Magic Flute, *also.*
¿No te interesan los deportes profesionales? No me interesan **tampoco**.	*You're not interested in professional sports? Me neither./I'm not interested in them either.*
Ese niño **siempre** hace travesuras.	*That boy is always doing mischief.*
Este niño no miente **nunca**.	*This boy never tells a lie.*

Spanish requires the use of double negatives if the negative clause begins with **no**. However, the negative forms can also be placed at the beginning of the clause. When this is done, the word **no** must be omitted. Compare the following examples:

Ella **no** lo haría **jamás/nunca**.	*She would never do that.*
Ella **jamás/nunca** lo haría.	
Esto **no** nos parece justo **tampoco**.	*This doesn't seem fair to us either.*
Tampoco esto nos parece justo.	
No hay **nadie** en la línea.	*There is no one/nobody on the (phone) line.*
Nadie hay en la línea.	

Cualquiera

If you search in a bilingual dictionary for the translation of *anyone* or *anybody*, you'll find **cualquiera** and **cualquier**, as well as **alguien** and its corresponding negative form **nadie** for *no one* or *nobody*. However, **cualquier(a)** and **alguien** are not interchangeable and in some cases, an error in usage can be insulting.

When you wish to say *anybody* or *anyone at all*, use the pronoun **cualquiera**:

Cualquiera te puede ayudar con esto.	*Anybody can help you with this.*

When **cualquiera** is used as an adjective, the final **-a** is dropped and the resulting form **cualquier** is placed before the noun it modifies, no matter what the gender:

Cualquier persona en el banco sabe esto.	*Anybody in the bank knows that.*

The plural forms of **cualquier** and **cualquiera** are, respectively, **cualesquier** and **cualesquiera**:

Lléveme **cualesquier** artículos que tengas sobre esto.	*Bring me any and all articles about this that you may have.*
Cualesquiera que sean sus motivos, Juan no es capaz de realizar el proyecto.	*Whatever his reasons are, John isn't capable of carrying out the project.*

Still another solution, when the notion of *anyone* is applied with the sense of *whosoever* or *whomsoever*, is **quienquiera**:

Quienquiera que crea esto es ingenuo.	*Anyone who believes this is naïve.*
Cuénteselo a **quienquiera**; mejor aún que todo el mundo lo sepa.	*Tell it to whomsoever; better still for the whole world to know about it.*

Observe that when you need to ask a question using *anyone*, such as when you are looking for someone, **alguien** is used:

¿Conoces a **alguien** que sepa crear un blog?	*Do you know anyone who knows how to create a blog?*

Finally, use extreme caution with **cualquiera**. If it modifies a noun or pronoun referring to a woman, it is unforgivably insulting. When used to refer to a man, **cualquiera** is depreciatory in various ways. The following sentence indicates that the man referred to is worthless on the job—the logic being that to be just *anybody* is the same as being *nobody*, that there is nothing distinguishing about him. The second sentence offers another way to say the same thing, the title of **don**, otherwise quite respectful, is juxtaposed with an insult—a common creative device for forming Spanish insults.

Ese señor Acero es **un tipo cualquiera**.	*That Mr. Acero fellow is a nobody.*
Ese señor Acero es **un don nadie**.	*That Mr. Acero is Sir Nobody.*

EJERCICIO 15·1

Match the word(s) in the second column with the correct translation in the first column.

_____ 1. also

_____ 2. no one/nobody

_____ 3. never

_____ 4. anyone

_____ 5. someone

_____ 6. none/not one

_____ 7. always

_____ 8. some

_____ 9. not either

_____ 10. something

_____ 11. nothing

_____ 12. whosoever

a. cualquiera

b. siempre

c. alguien

d. nadie

e. tampoco

f. quienquiera

g. algo

h. nunca/jamás

i. ningún

j. algún

k. también

l. nada

EJERCICIO 15·2

Select the option that correctly completes the numbered items to show the use of indefinite and negative words.

1. A Juan no le gustan los guisantes...

   a. ...y nosotros los comemos.

   b. ...a mí tampoco me gustan.

   c. ...y yo los como también.

2. Necesito ayuda para hacer una compra.

   a. ¿Habrá algún dependiente en la tienda quien me pueda servir?

   b. Hay una oferta buena.

   c. ¿Se ofrecen descuentos?

3. El niño no se duerme fácilmente.

   a. ¿Tendrá un poco de hambre también?

   b. Es que no quiere dormir la siesta nunca.

   c. Tiene sueño.

4. Abrí la puerta al oír que alguien tocaba, pero...

    a. ...había tres personas esperándome también.

    b. ...no sonó el timbre tampoco.

    c. ...no había nadie allí.

5. Fui a buscar, pero no había...

    a. ...alguna copa.

    b. ...copa ninguna.

    c. ...copa alguna.

6. Creo que hay ... en la cocina.

    a. alguna que otra copa

    b. ninguna copa

    c. nada

7. ...que oiga esto diría que el Sr. Acero es insensato.

    a. Alguien

    b. Quienquiera

    c. Cualquier

8. No hay ... en la clase.

    a. alguien

    b. algunos alumnos

    c. nadie

9. Vino ... muchacha para visitarte, Juan.

    a. alguna

    b. algún

    c. algunas

10. No lo he visto...

    a. también

    b. siempre

    c. nunca

11. Juana no toca los tambores, ... yo...

    a. o ... tampoco

    b. y ... también

    c. ni ... tampoco

12. ...cuando íbamos a la playa, nos quemábamos. ¡Ay!

    a. Nunca

    b. Siempre

    c. Jamás

13. ...ingeniero sabe que la piedra resiste la compresión más que la madera.

    a. Quienquiera

    b. Cualquier

    c. Cualquiera

14. No sé si hay ... esperando a la puerta.

    a. algún

    b. nadie

    c. alguien

15. ...nado ... porque no traje traje.

    a. Ninguno ... nadie

    b. No ... nada

    c. Algo ... también

16. Ese fármaco no surtió efecto...

    a. algo

    b. ningún

    c. alguno

17. ...sabe a ciencia cierta si hay vida en otros planetas, aunque parece probable.

    a. Cualquiera

    b. Algunos

    c. Nadie

18. ...le puede informar sobre los precios de ida y vuelta.

   a. Nada

   b. Cualquiera

   c. Algo

19. Jorge no había viajado en tren...

   a. siempre

   b. también

   c. jamás

20. ...tenían interés en ese cuento, pero a la mayoría de las alumnas, no les llamaba la atención.

   a. Alguien

   b. Algunas

   c. Algunos

Translate the following sentences from English to Spanish.

1. Is there anyone here who can help me?

   _____

2. I don't want to eat pizza either.

   _____

3. There isn't a single cracker on the tray. (don't use **"ni una galleta"**)

   _____

4. Do you have some wine that is really good? (**Uds.**)

   _____

5. The coffee was never ready on time.

   _____

6. Someone called for you this morning. (**tú**)

   _____

7. I don't know anyone who has climbed that mountain.

   _____

8. No one has climbed that mountain. (give two possible constructions, one of which requires the subjunctive)

_____

9. Any doctor can tell you that! (**tú**)

_____

10. Some salesman left you this sample. (**tú**)

_____

11. No one in this class reads more than I do. (give two possible constructions, one of which requires the subjunctive)

_____

12. I read more than anyone in this class.

_____

13. Anybody who believes Mr. Acero is crazy.

_____

14. I don't know anybody who can do that either. (give two possible constructions, both of which require the subjunctive)

_____

15. No one is home. (give two constructions: one with **estar**, one with **hay**)

_____

16. He likes to ride bicycles too.

_____

17. They never used to go to that restaurant. (give two possible constructions, neither of which involve the subjunctive, but rather the placement of the negative word)

_____

18. There's something that is bothering her.

_____

19. It was nothing; just a little gift.

_____

20. Don't you *ever* go to the beach?! (give two possible constructions, neither of which involve the subjunctive, but rather the placement of the negative word)

_____

Relative pronouns

As the term suggests, relative pronouns are *pronouns* that stand in for a noun and *relative* in that they stand in for a previously mentioned noun, known as an *antecedent*. The relative pronouns in English are *that, who, whom* (the form used when *who* is an object instead of subject), and *which*. These words are used to join shorter sentences or clauses when the first sentence or clause has a subject or object that is subject or object of the second sentence.

A relative pronoun functions as a conjunction, such as *and*. Consider the following pair of sentences:

> He bought three cars. They were antiques.
> He bought three cars *and* they were antiques.

Now observe how these two sentences can be joined more elegantly using *that* or, in some dialects of English, *which*:

> He bought three cars that were antiques.
> The three cars that/which he bought were antiques.
> Of course, you could also say:
> He bought three antique cars.

The function of relative pronouns in Spanish is the same as in English. In Spanish, there are only five relative pronouns in common usage. If you don't count the plurals of two of them as separate forms, there are only *three* high-frequency relative pronouns in Spanish:

que	*that, who, whom*
quien, quienes	*who*
cual, cuales	*which*

Note in passing that the forms **cuyo, cuyos, cuya** and **cuyas**—all meaning *whose*—tend to be more common in literature but are occasionally heard in speech. They are adjectives agreeing with the noun they modify:

El hombre **cuya madre** vivía en Lima nos llamó anoche.	*The man whose mother used to live in Lima called us last night.*

Whenever an antecedent is human, the relative pronouns **que** or **quien/quienes** may be used. The only difference between the use of **quien** and **que** is that **quien** is more formal; but **quien** only can be used for human subjects or objects of a relative clause.

Conozco a los maestros **que** se jubilaron el año pasado.	*I know the teachers who/that retired last year.*

When a preposition is needed, **quien**, not **que**, must be used:

Conozco a los maestros con **quienes** te jubilaste el año pasado.	*I know the teachers you retired with last year.*
Los tres hombres **que** fueron a Miami decidieron tomar un vuelo a Bogotá.	*The three men that/who went to Miami decided to take a flight to Bogotá.*
Las hijas del Sr. Gómez **que** participaron en el concurso fueron a Maracaibo.	*Mr. Gomez's daughters who participated in the contest went to Maracaibo.*
Los grabados de Goya **que** se exhibieron ayer eran muy perturbadores.	*The engravings of Goya that were exhibited yesterday were very disturbing.*

The relative clauses in the last two examples above are *restrictive*. That is, the listener can conclude that Mr. Gomez has other daughters who did *not* participate in the contest and that there were other engravings of Goya exhibited yesterday that were *not* disturbing. However, by placing commas around the relative clause (and pausing appropriately in speech), the listener will know that Mr. Gomez has no other daughters and that, therefore, all his daughters went to Maracaibo, and that, although there may be other engravings by Goya, all the ones exhibited yesterday were disturbing. Here are the same sentences, but the relative clauses are now *non-restrictive*:

Las hijas del Sr. Gómez, **quienes/que** participaron en el concurso, fueron a Maracaibo.	*Mr. Gomez's daughters, who participated in the contest, went to Maracaibo.*
Los grabados de Goya, **que** se exhibieron ayer, eran muy perturbadores.	*The engravings of Goya, which were exhibited yesterday, were very disturbing.*

The form **cual/cuales** is more formal than **que** and, like **que**, they can refer either to human or non-human subjects or objects. As can be the case with **que**, the word **cual** is used with **el** and **la**, while **cuales** is used with **los** and **las**. In the last example, the commas enclose the non-restrictive clause to show that all the groom's friends participated in the wedding—none were left out.

De todos los participantes, **los que** llegaron en primer lugar tenían más de 40 años.	*Among all the participants, those that/who came in first were over 40 years old.*
Entrevistaron a varias personas, entre **las cuales** figuraban los asesores del Primer Ministro.	*They interviewed various people, among whom were advisors of the Prime Minister.*
Los amigos del novio, **los cuales** participaron en la boda, le compraron un carro nuevo.	*The friends of the groom, who participated in the wedding, bought him a new car.*

The combination **lo que** and **lo cual** both translate as *the thing which*, and both come in quite handy:

Se cortó la comunicación, **lo que/cual** resultó en demoras en los vuelos a Buenos Aires.	*The communications were cut, which resulted in delays of flights to Buenos Aires.*

If the relative pronoun refers to a human, either **que** or **quien** may be used, as the following example shows. Observe first how the two sentences become one by uniting them with, in this case, either relative pronoun:

El hombre cruzó la calle. Llevaba un sombrero negro.	*The man crossed the street. He wore a black hat.*
El hombre, **que/quien** cruzó la calle, llevaba un sombrero negro.	*The man, who crossed the street, wore a black hat.*

However, if the relative pronoun refers to a human and involves a preposition, **quien** *must* be used. In the following examples, notice that a preposition is used, and that the preposition comes before the relative pronoun **quien**. The last pair of sentences shows how, in English, the preposition can, and often does, come at the end of a clause, but this pattern must never be imitated in Spanish.

El amigo **a quien** llamé vino a la fiesta.	*The friend that/whom I called came to the party.*
Los clientes **de quienes** recibí la comisión decidieron cambiar de banco.	*The customers that I got a commission from decided to change banks.*
Cuando regresé de España, no tenía **con quién** hablar español.	*When I returned from Spain, I didn't have anyone to speak Spanish to/with.*

For non-human objects, **que** (never **quien**) is used as the relative pronoun. Notice that the word *that* may be omitted in English. However, the relative pronoun can *never* be omitted in Spanish:

El perro **que** compramos fue muy leal.	*The dog (that) we bought was very loyal.*
La casa **que** pintaron se construyó en el siglo XIX.	*The house (that) they painted was built in the nineteenth century.*

EJERCICIO
16·1

Connect the following pairs of sentences using the proper relative pronouns. When there is more than one possibility, write both.

1. Veo al hombre. Él compró un auto ayer.

_____

2. ¿Conoces a las chicas? Les diste unos dulces.

_____

3. El Sr. Acero mintió. Esto le va a causar muchos problemas.

_____

4. Hablé con tu hermano. Hice un favor para él.

_____

5. Acabo de ver de nuevo a Teresa. Fui con ella al cine la semana pasada.

_____

6. Los niños juegan al escondite. Es un juego muy popular.

_____

7. ¿Viste a ese policía? Me puso una multa.

_____

8. Voy a llamar a las tres chicas. Salieron de clase temprano.

_____

9. Conozco bien a Tomás. Te hablé mucho sobre él anoche.

_____

10. Leyeron las noticias de ayer. No les gustó.

_____

11. Tengo un perro. Sabe muchos trucos.

_____

12. Vamos a buscar al dependiente. Él te ofreció un descuento anoche.

_____

13. Subimos una escalera. No está bien iluminada.

_____

14. Ellos compraron la casa. Tiene un patio amplio.

_____

15. Vi a uno de las hijas de la Sra. Gómez. Ella tiene el pelo liso.

_____

16. ¿Quieres acompañarme al parque? Tiene columpios.

_____

17. Juan vendió la heladería. No manejaban paletas en ésa.

_____

18. ¿Compraste el pastel? Tenía cerezas encima.

_____

19. ¿Viste el gato? Tenía un ojo verde y el otro amarillo.

_____

20. Tienes una computadora. Funciona bien.

_____

Translate the following sentences from English to Spanish.

1. I don't know the man whom you're talking about. (**Ud.**)

   _____

2. She brought me soup, which made me happy.

   _____

3. We sold the car that didn't run well.

   _____

4. They called Mr. Gonzalez's son, who is a doctor.

   _____

5. Did you see the game that he wrote about in the newspaper? (**tú**)

   _____

6. Of the three boys who were running, the one who fell down is my younger brother.

   _____

7. His three large dogs that won the contest are all four years old.

   _____

8. He went to the movie, even though he didn't have anyone to go with him.

   _____

9. The box he brought was empty.

   _____

10. The man whom I saw was tall and wore a gray suit.

    _____

11. The manager whose store was closed decided to quit.

    _____

12. The woman I got a message from did not return my call.

    _____

13. Her mother, who is from France, bought me a bottle of wine.

    _____

14. We interviewed five candidates, among whom only one was bilingual.

    _____

15. Her sisters who went to see the movie went home early.

    _____

16. Their friends, who had read the novel, liked the book club very much.

_____

17. The ones I liked I invited to the concert.

_____

18. The wine, which was in boxes, was sent to the restaurant.

_____

19. Do you know the man whose wife is president of her own company? (**Uds.**)

_____

20. We saw the woman we got the present from.

_____

Subordinated clauses

There is one word in Spanish that seems to turn up everywhere—the word **que**. This word has many functions and is translated into English in various ways, depending on the grammatical job it performs in any particular sentence. Sometimes it means *that, who,* or *which,* as we saw in the previous chapter on relative pronouns. In comparisons, **que** means *than.* Other times, it can't be translated at all, but it has to be in the Spanish phrase, such as in **hacer** *time clauses* or in the formula of obligation formed by **tener** + **que** + infinitive. Last but not least, don't forget that **¿qué?** (note the accent mark!) is the Spanish interrogative meaning *what?*

In this chapter you will see another way that simple sentences can be joined to form more complex ones and how, often, various tenses of the subjunctive mood must be used for verbs in subordinated clauses. This chapter will examine subordinated noun, adjective, and adverbial clauses and make some additional observations about sequence of tense. First, let's review some definitions.

In order for a clause to be subordinated, there has to be some principal clause to introduce it. Another name for the principal clause is *independent clause*; likewise, the subordinated clause is also known as the *dependent clause.* Observe how the following two independent sentences can be combined. In the first combined or more complex sentence, the result is a relative clause. In the second example, the second of the two joined sentences has become a subordinated noun clause.

I saw the boy. The boy climbed the tree.

↓

I saw the boy that/who climbed the tree.

↓

I saw that the boy climbed the tree.

The relative clause *describes* the boy. The portion of the sentence beginning with *that* (or *who*) all the way to the end of the sentence functions as a giant *adjective.* In the third sentence, the portion of the sentence beginning with *that* to the end of the sentence functions as a giant *direct object* of the verb *saw*—the verb in the main clause. Here the relative clause tells the reader or listener *what* the subject of the independent clause (*I*) *saw.* The phrase *that the boy climbed the tree* can't stand alone as a grammatical sentence; it has been subordinated to the main clause *I saw,* which can stand alone. Notice that each clause in the third sentence has its own subject and its own conjugated verb. Here is an example of a sentence in which all the subjects are implicit since the verb endings clearly tell us who the subjects are. Remember that whereas the word *that* can be omitted in English, the conjunction **que** can never be omitted in Spanish:

Veo **que** escribes una carta.	*I see (that) you're writing a letter.*

The structure of subordinated noun clauses can be stated in formulaic terms. Observe the following formula wherein S = *subject* and V = *verb*. The subscripted numbers remind us that the subjects of the two clauses are different and that each has its own verb.

$$S_1 + V_1 + \textbf{que} + S_2 + V_2$$

This formula is very valuable when we apply one more mnemonic (memory) trick for telling us when a subjunctive form of the verb in the subordinated clause must be used. The mnemonic is W.I.E.R.D.O. and the letters stand for types of verbs in the V_1 position that will require the subjunctive be used for verbs in the V_2 position. Let's unpack what the acronym W.I.E.R.D.O. stands for and then see some examples.

- **W** Wanting, wishing, hoping, expecting
- **I** Impersonal expressions of any of the other letters in this acronym (**es** + adjective)
- **E** Emotion
- **R** Requests, requirements, orders, commands, petitions
- **D** Doubt, denial, negation
- **O** Ojalá

In English, the most frequently used structure that corresponds in meaning to the Spanish in the **W** and **R** categories of the acronym is verb + object + infinitive. This structure makes no sense whatsoever in Spanish, so observe carefully the differences and similarities between the structure of Spanish and the English translations in the following examples. The examples are listed in order of the categories represented by the acronym:

Quieren **que tú les ayudes.**	*They want you to help them.*
Es importante **que ellos vayan al gimnasio.**	*It's important (that) they go to the gym.*

However, if an impersonal expression does not correspond to any of the verb categories of the acronym, the *indicative* is used. In the following first example, the impersonal expression **es obvio** does not express a *wish*, *emotion*, *requirement*, or a *doubt*:

Es obvio que ellos van al gimnasio.	*It's obvious (that) they're going/they go to the gym.*
Juana **se alegra de que** su novio tenga un buen trabajo.	*Jane is glad (that) her boyfriend has a good job.*
El capitán **manda que** los tripulantes limpien la cubierta.	*The captain orders the crew to clean the deck.*
Los agnósticos **dudan que** Dios exista.	*Agnostics doubt that God exists.*

Furthermore, if a verb of belief is negated by using **no**, the subjunctive must be used:

No creo que el Sr. Acero **vaya** a admitirlo.	*I don't believe (that) Mr. Acero is going to admit it.*

Likewise, when a verb of doubt is undone by using **no**, the indicative must be used:

No dudo que el Sr. Acero **es** culpable de varios crímenes.	*I do not doubt (that) Mr. Acero is guilty of various crimes.*

Finally, *always* use the subjunctive with **ojalá**. The word **ojalá** is derived from Arabic and means, roughly, *May God (Allah) grant that* . . . or *May it please God (Allah) to*. . . . It is not necessary to use **que** when using **ojalá** because, interestingly, the original Arabic phrase already implied it. When translated into English, it comes out simplest by saying *I hope that*. . . .

Ojalá (que) Juan **venga** esta noche.	*I hope John's coming/John comes tonight.*

You may have been wondering what happens if the subjects of two sentences to be joined are the same person. When there is no change of subject, the new sentence is structured as in English:

I want. I dance.
What do I want to do?—I want to dance.

The structure is the same in Spanish, as the following examples show:

Yo quiero bailar.	*I want to dance.*
Me alegro de estar aquí.	*I'm glad to be here/about being here.*
Es importante bailar.	*It's important to dance.*

However, since a singular subject cannot logically command him- or herself, there is no example of the **R** category in which the subject of the main clause is also the subject of the dependent clause. The nearest one can come to that is the **nosotros** command (always expressed in the present subjunctive):

Cantemos.	*Let's sing.*

When verbs of doubt are involved, the rule about the subjects of the two clauses having to be different *can* be broken. However, the preference of the Royal Academy is to use the structure of the first form in the following example.

Dudo poder ir.	*I doubt I'll be able to go.*
Dudo que (yo) pueda ir.	

Before continuing to examine subordinated adjective clauses, you need to understand the concept of sequence of tense. First, examine the following series of examples that show the temporal logic of the use of the four tenses of the subjunctive mood. Since emotion can be felt now about actions in the present, past, or future, a verb of emotion in the present is used in the main clause to allow you to focus on what is happening in the subordinated clause:

Me alegro de que Juan **venga** esta noche.	*I'm glad John is coming tonight.*
Me alegro de que Juan **haya venido** a esta fiesta.	*I'm glad John has come to this party.*
Me alegro de que Juan **viniera** a la fiesta anoche.	*I'm glad John came to the party last night.*
Me da pena que Juan **no hubiera llegado** a tiempo para conocer a María.	*I'm so sorry John hadn't arrived in time to meet Mary.*

When the main verb in a sentence containing a subordinated clause is in the present, the present or present perfect subjunctive is used. If the main verb is in the past, then the imperfect or the imperfect subjunctive is used.

Juan **espera** que María lo **llame**.	*John hopes Mary will call him.*
Juan **esperaba** que María lo **llamara**.	*John hoped Mary would call him.*
Ellos le **dicen*** que **ponga** la ropa en la maleta.	*The tell him/her/you formal to put the clothes in the suitcase.*
Ellos le **dijeron** que **pusiera** la ropa en la maleta.	*They told him/her/you formal to put the clothes in the suitcase.*
Es raro que **no haya nevado** todavía.	*It's odd that it hasn't snowed yet.*

Subordinated adjective clauses are clauses that describe a noun or pronoun mentioned in the main, or independent clause. In the following example, the clause **que se fabricó en Suiza** is a giant adjective and could be replaced by using the adjective **suizo**. The fact that the whole clause could be replaced by one adjective proves that it is an adjective clause and not a noun clause. It is important to make the distinction, since the rules governing the requirement of the subjunctive in subordinated adjective clauses are different from the rules used with subordinated noun clauses.

Tengo un reloj **que se fabricó en Suiza**.	*I have a watch that was made in Switzerland.*
Tengo un reloj **suizo**.	*I have a Swiss watch.*

The subjunctive must be used in a subordinated adjective clause if the antecedent, or previously mentioned noun (**reloj**, in the example), is vague or doesn't exist. Let's change the example to require the subjunctive in the subordinated clause:

Busco un reloj que **sea** suizo.	*I'm looking for a watch that's Swiss.*

Of course, you could simply say **Busco un reloj suizo**—but there are times when one needs subordinated adjective clauses (and the subjunctive as well). This example simply shows how they are constructed. Here are a couple more examples that also show sequence of tense in action:

No hay relojes en esta tienda que **vengan** de Suiza.	*There are no watches in this shop that come from Switzerland.*
No había relojes en esa tienda que **vinieran** de Suiza.	*There were no watches in that shop that came from Switzerland.*
Necesito un reloj que **tenga** una manecilla para marcar los segundos.	*I need a watch that has a hand for showing the seconds.*
Necesitaba un reloj que **tuviera** una manecilla para marcar los segundos.	*I needed a watch that had a hand for showing the seconds.*

***decir**, as in *to tell* someone to do something

Some students have been told that if the indefinite article is used before the antecedent in the main clause, the subjunctive must be used in the adjective clause. This is often true, but as often it is not. Both the verb and the article of the main clause must be taken into account. In other words, pay attention to the meaning of the whole situation as expressed by the whole sentence, as these examples illustrate:

Busco un carro que **tenga** GPS.	*I'm looking for a car that has GPS.*
Buscaba un carro que **tuviera** GPS.	*I was looking for a car that had GPS.*

But:

Tengo un carro que **tiene** GPS.	*I have a car that has GPS.*
Tenía un carro que **tenía** GPS.	*I had a car that had GPS.*
Busco la secretaria que **sabe** alemán.	*I'm looking for the secretary that/who speaks German.*
Buscaba la secretaria que **sabía** alemán.	*I was looking for the secretary that/who spoke German.*

The best way to approach the use of adverbial expressions to form more complex sentences is to observe from the outset that some adverbial expressions are *always* followed by a verb in the subjunctive and others only *sometimes* are followed by a verb in the subjunctive.

The subjunctive is always used after the following expressions:

a menos que, a no ser que	*unless*
antes de que	*before*
como si (+ imperfect subjunctive)	*as if*
con tal de que, siempre y cuando	*provided that, as long as*
en caso de que	*in case that*
el hecho de que	*the fact that*
para que, a fin de que	*in order that*
sin que	*without*

After the following expressions, the subjunctive is sometimes used:

a pesar de que	*despite, in spite of*
acaso, tal vez, quizá	*perhaps*
así que, así como	*such that*
aunque	*although*
cuando	*when*
de modo que, de manera que	*in such a way that*
después de que, luego que	*after*
hasta que	*until*
mientras	*while*
por más que, por mucho que	*no matter how much*
siempre que	*as long as*
tan pronto como, en cuanto	*as soon as*
una vez que	*once you have*

One of the best ways to learn how to use the subjunctive correctly (when faced with an expression on the second list) is to remember the following three examples. Observe that when a time clause is involved, the subjunctive must be used if the action is—or was—anticipated.

Vamos a la tienda **después de que** deje de llover.	*We'll go to the store after it quits raining.*
Fuimos a la tienda **después de que** dejó de llover.	*We went to the store after it quit raining.*
Íbamos a ir a la tienda **después de que** dejara de llover.	*We were going to go to the store after it quit raining.*

The problem then is how to determine whether the subjunctive is needed after the adverbial expressions in the second list. Just as we have the W.E.I.R.D.O. acronym to help us deal with subordinated noun clauses, and the idea of vague or non-existent antecedents to guide our choice with subordinated adjective clauses, the use of the subjunctive after the expressions in the second list of adverbial expressions is decided by whether the action(s) following the expressions are or were anticipated or whether the action is a mere report of an action in the past.

In concrete terms, if the main verb is in the past, the time frame of the whole sentence is in the past. There is no anticipation and, therefore, the subjunctive is not used. When the main verb is in the present, actions following the adverbial expressions are (or were) anticipated and, therefore, verbs following the expressions must be in the subjunctive. Among the expressions in the second list, the expressions **acaso**, **tal vez**, and **quizá** (*perhaps*) and **aunque** (*although*) are the only ones in which the use of the subjunctive or indicative depends on the attitude of the speaker, to show more or less certainty.

It is important to understand the concept of sequence of tense when dealing with the subjunctive generally, but for some students this is particularly tricky when dealing with adverbial expressions. Observe the following contrastive examples, noting how the subjunctive is used when the element of anticipation is present and the indicative is used (second example) when the action following the adverbial expression is a mere report. Note too that the tense of the subjunctive is present if the main verb is in the present, as in the first and third examples, but imperfect subjunctive when the main verb is in the past and the expression requires the subjunctive, as in the last example.

Vamos al parque después de que **deje** de llover.	*We'll go to the park after it quits raining.*
Fuimos al parque después de que **dejó** de llover.	*We went to the park after it quit raining.*
Vamos al parque antes de que **empiece** a llover.	*Let's go the park before it rains.*
Fuimos al parque antes de que **empezara** a llover.	*We went to the park before it started to rain.*

The following translation exercises will challenge you to create various types of subordinated clauses. The first set, from Spanish to English, is intended to sensitize you, to enable you to recognize the various types of subordinated clauses. The second will require you to create them in Spanish. Remember, in English, the conjunction *that* can be omitted! In both, the issue of sequence of tense will be addressed.

Translate the following sentences from Spanish to English.

1. Era dudoso que mis primos hubieran preparado la cena cuando mi papá llegó.

   _____

2. Creo que es posible que llueva mañana.

   _____

3. Buscábamos una escopeta que tuviera dos cañones.

   _____

4. Mi papá tenía un jardín que producía muchos tomates.

   _____

5. Cuando decidas si vas a ir conmigo o no, me llamarás, ¿no?

   _____

6. Venderá el auto con tal de que se le ofrezca por lo menos quinientos dólares.

   _____

7. Los niños esperan que todos nosotros juguemos al fútbol.

   _____

8. Es preciso que tú y yo lleguemos a un acuerdo.

   _____

9. Los tres querían que yo me quedara en casa hasta que dejara de llover.

   _____

10. Es curioso que ella siempre haya insistido en que yo no la llamara los fines de semana.

    _____

11. Por mucho que le rogáramos que nos prestara el dinero, él no quiso prestárnoslo.

    _____

12. Necesitamos un programa que nos permita procesar más datos en menos tiempo.

    _____

13. Ella tiene un novio que la quiere mucho.

    _____

14. Dudamos que los padres de Enrique hayan olvidado su cumpleaños.

    _____

15. Ellos se alegran de que tú no hayas dejado los estudios.

_____

16. Te ruego que me llames antes de que se cierre el mercado.

_____

17. ¿Quieres que te busque una película que no sea de terror?

_____

18. Después de que se bañó, Juan se vistió y se fue.

_____

19. Antes de que saliera de casa, Juan se bañó y se vistió.

_____

20. Es imposible que ella no lo supiera antes de la fiesta.

_____

_____

EJERCICIO
17·2

Translate the following sentences from English to Spanish.

1. Her mother is glad you have seen the play. (**tú**)

_____

2. We went to the store before our father came home.

_____

3. Do you want me to read the story to you? (**tú**)

_____

4. She and I needed to find a car that had a CD player.

_____

5. Are you worried the computer doesn't have enough memory? (**tú**)

_____

6. Did they ask you to bring the report? (**Uds.**)

_____

7. They needed to find a pharmacy that was open twenty-four hours.

_____

8. We know you have written the letters to him. (**tú**)

_____

9. They are sure he had seen the movie before their mother returned home.

_____

10. It was important he finish the race.

_____

11. It is doubtful Catherine has published, or will publish, an article.

_____

12. She required her students to have five written pages by the end of every week.

_____

13. It was a miracle he hadn't drowned.

_____

14. It was obvious that her mother had not wanted her to come to our party.

_____

15. They promised us they would help us, provided we pay them in advance.

_____

16. If you asked me to do you a favor, I would do it for you. (**tú**)

_____

17. After you have finished breakfast, we can go to the zoo. (**Uds.**)

_____

18. It's good you're going to the concert! (**tú**)

_____

19. She entered the house again without her parents' knowing it.

_____

20. We saw the salesman who had sold us the car.

_____

Pero, sino, sino que, and other sentence-building devices

Pero, sino, sino que

When English-speaking learners of Spanish encounter problems with this group of expressions, it is because they think they all mean *but*—and that the use of **pero** matches the use of *but* in English. However, while **pero** does mean *but*, it is not interchangeable with the uses of **sino**, which means *but rather*. The phrase **sino que** also means *but rather*; however, it is used when followed by a conjugated verb.

The word **pero** is used in an affirmative statement to add to or redirect the information immediately preceding it. **Pero** joins two clauses whose information is related to each other. In the following examples, the information that follows **pero** does not contradict what precedes it. In the first example, the fact that they are going to eat does not mean that they aren't going to the movies—they're simply going to eat before they go. In the second example, nothing about John's being tired contradicts his value as a worker. The word **pero** is used when the introductory clause is an *affirmative* statement and when what follows does not contradict or correct what precedes it, but adds to it in some way:

Vamos al cine **pero** primero tenemos que comer.	*We're going to the movie theater but first we have to eat.*
Juan parece estar cansado **pero** trabaja bien.	*John seems tired **but** he works well.*

However, if the introductory statement is negative, then **sino** (*but rather*) is used. The difference between **pero** and **sino** is that the information that **sino** adds contradicts or corrects the information in the preceding statement. Notice in the following examples how this contradictory or correcting information is presented by contrasting nouns, adjectives, or infinitives; thus, after **sino**, no conjugated verb is used.

No fue a **clase sino al gimnasio.**	*He didn't go to class but (rather) to the gym.*
Elena no es **baja sino alta.**	*Helen isn't short but (rather) tall.*
No queríamos **bailar sino ver** una película.	*We didn't want to dance, but rather to see a movie.*

If the new, contradictory, or correcting information introduced by **sino** requires a conjugated verb, then and only then, **que** must follow **sino**. Remember that one function of **que** is to link a sentence to a previous one. The second sentence is then a subordinated clause and that clause, by definition, contains conjugated verbs. Unlike the previous example that uses an infinitive as the point of contrast, the first clause in the following examples concludes with a conjugated verb.

Mi hermano no **corre sino que nada.**	*My brother doesn't run, but rather he swims.*
El Sr. Acero **no es amable sino que maltrata** a todos sus colegas.	*Mr. Acero isn't friendly, but rather he mistreats all his colleagues.*
Su hija **no estudia mucho sino que pierde** el tiempo leyendo tiras cómicas.	*Her daughter doesn't study much, but rather she wastes her time reading comic strips.*

Other constructions

In addition to knowing how to form relative clauses, subordinate clauses, and conjunctions such as **que, pero**, and **sino**, there are other constructions that will make your command of Spanish much more native-like. Here are a few more ways to make your Spanish more interesting and engaging, encouraging native speakers to converse with you.

There are two constructions involving **sino** that mean *not only . . . but*:

No sólo vino Juan **sino** María también.	*Not only John came, but also Mary.*
Juan no tan sólo comió el pollo **sino que** bebió todo el vino.	*John not only ate the chicken but he drank all the wine.*

The common English correlative *either . . . or* is rendered in Spanish by **o ... o**:

Creo que **o** vamos a ganar **o** vamos a quedar empatados.	*I think we're either going to win or end in a tie.*

The corresponding negative form of the foregoing correlative, *neither . . . nor* is rendered in Spanish as **ni ... ni**:

Ni tú **ni** él tienen la menor idea de qué va a pasar mañana.	*Neither you nor he has the least idea about what is going to happen tomorrow.*

A handy and frequently encountered temporal correlative, corresponding to the English *from . . . until* is rendered as **desde ... hasta**:

Los obreros estuvieron aquí **desde** las siete de la mañana **hasta** las cuatro de la tarde.	*The workers were here from seven in the morning until four in the afternoon.*

Another formula, corresponding to the English phrase for expressing the ratios *the more (or less) . . . the more (or less)* is rendered as **cuanto más/menos ... tanto más/menos**. The word **tanto** can often be omitted in speech:

Cuanto más estudio esto, **(tanto) menos** lo entiendo.	*The more I study this, the less I understand it.*
Cuanto más Juan escucha la pieza de Mozart, **(tanto) más** le parece una maravilla.	*The more John listens to the Mozart piece, the more marvelous it seems to him.*

When two comparative or contrastive clauses are of equal importance, use the formula **tanto ... como** meaning *as well (as)* or, even more simply but less elegantly, *and*:

El soldado sabía tanto manejar las armas como usar el equipo de comunicaciones.

Me gusta el ajedrez **tanto como** las damas.

The soldier knew how to use the weapons as well as how to use the communications equipment.

I like chess as much as I like dominoes.

EJERCICIO
18·1

Fill in the blanks with **pero**, **sino**, *or* **sino que**, *as appropriate.*

1. Sé que llueve, _____ vamos a hacer una caminata en las montañas.

2. Juan no es perezoso, _____ muy trabajador.

3. María no canta, _____ nada.

4. Los niños no desean estudiar, _____ jugar en el patio.

5. Éstos no son libros, _____ artículos.

6. Los huéspedes no cantaban *karaoke*, _____ jugaban a dardos.

7. A mi papá no le gusta cazar tanto ahora, _____ pescar.

8. Decidí salir a dar un paseo, _____ primero tuve que lavar los platos.

9. La lámpara no se cayó, _____ se apagó de repente.

10. Catherine y Micaela no escribían nada, _____ asistían a presentaciones y chismeaban.

11. No regué el jardín, _____ limpié el garaje.

12. Ella es de la Florida, _____ su esposo es de Nueva York.

13. No nos desayunamos con fruta, _____ con pan tostado, mermelada y café.

14. Juana sí está a dieta, _____ no hace ejercicios.

15. Me encanta la literatura, _____ lo que más me agrada es leer biografías e historia.

16. Gabriel García Márquez no es argentino, _____ colombiano.

17. Mi amigo peruano no estudiaba la ingeniería, _____ tomaba clases de arquitectura.

18. Es un submarino, sí, _____ la Marina lo retiró de servicio.

19. No navega el barco, _____ vuela sobre las olas.

20. Él es amigable, _____ no tan dadivoso.

Translate the following sentences from English to Spanish.

1. We want to work in the garden but it is raining.

   _____

2. He doesn't have a computer, but a typewriter.

   _____

3. We aren't drinking coffee, but tea.

   _____

4. My friends were not working, but sleeping!

   _____

5. He went fishing, but didn't catch one!

   _____

6. She didn't want to fix dinner, but rather watch a movie and order pizza.

   _____

7. Neither Mary nor John went to the party.

   _____

8. The more I listen to classical music, the more I like it.

   _____

9. She not only read the newspaper, but all the magazines too.

   _____

10. It will either rain or snow tomorrow.

    _____

11. The less he read, the dumber he seemed to others.

    _____

12. It isn't gold, but silver.

    _____

13. The moon isn't made of cheese, but it is yellow.

    _____

14. She lived in Panama from 1990 until 2000.

    _____

15. My friends and I cook as much as we eat.

    _____

16. He didn't call her, but rather he wrote her a letter.

_____

17. Nowadays, people don't write letters, but rather everyone sends each other text messages.

_____

18. Daniel didn't come in the front door, but rather the back.

_____

19. He will either fly or take a train to Montevideo.

_____

20. I don't want eggs or bacon.

_____

Calendar dates, time, and phone numbers

This chapter deals with the conventions for expressing dates, the time, phone numbers, and addresses. Knowing these conventions will enable you to function socially with less confusion.

When analog clocks became available in wristwatch size, more variety began to appear in how people would report what time it was. For instance, when looking at an analog display reading of 1:15, it makes more sense to say *one-fifteen* than *a quarter-past one*, although both are correct. This usage is also more common today since cell phones are now our primary mode of finding out the time.

Likewise, when the year 2000 rolled around, there was discussion in the English-speaking world about how we would express the year after 2010. Would we say *twenty-ten* or *two-thousand ten*? The matter is not settled for English speakers, but it seems likely that beginning in 2020, English speakers will revert to the two-digit manner of stating the year and we will say *twenty twenty, twenty twenty-one*, and so forth. There was no such discussion in the Spanish-speaking world about how to express the year because in Spanish, the year has always been stated just as any other number (e.g., **dos mil**, **dos mil uno**). So, in the year 2020, Spanish speakers will simply say **dos mil veinte** and not **veinte-veinte**—*unless* the latter becomes briefly fashionable because of the digital and verbal symmetry of that particular year.

Let's begin with the days of the week, hours of the day, months, and seasons—all of which you certainly already know as vocabulary items. Knowing the gender of these nouns is important in order to correctly express more detailed data, whether in speech or when doing something simple such as filling out a form or recording the date.

The days of the week are:

lunes	*Monday*
martes	*Tuesday*
miércoles	*Wednesday*
jueves	*Thursday*
viernes	*Friday*
sábado	*Saturday*
domingo	*Sunday*

The months of the year are:

enero	*January*
febrero	*February*
marzo	*March*
abril	*April*

mayo	*May*
junio	*June*
julio	*July*
agosto	*August*
septiembre*	*September*
octubre	*October*
noviembre	*November*
diciembre	*December*

Keep in mind that the days and months are masculine because the words **día** and **mes** are masculine: **el día, el mes**. Unlike English, the names of the days of the week and the months are not capitalized in Spanish, except on a wall calendar or in a heading. One trick for remembering that days and months both are masculine is to visualize a calendar because it displays the *days* of each *month*. The use of the article **el** before the name of a day of the week means *on* that day; when used in the plural, it means *on* all the days of that same name. However, the article **el** is not used before the names of months to mean "in" that month; to say *in March*, Spanish says, like English, **en marzo**. When referring to a month more remote in time, use **en el mes de** … .This also is important when speaking of the past, since the preterit and imperfect are involved:

Mi tía vino **el lunes**.	*My aunt came on Monday.*
Mi tía venía **los lunes**.	*My aunt would come (habitually) on Mondays.*
En marzo, volvieron las golondrinas.	*In March, the swallows returned.*
En diciembre, Amanda cumplirá treinta años.	*In December, Amanda will turn thirty.*
Ese año, **en el mes de abril**, comenzó la guerra.	*That year, in the month of April, the war began.*

The hours of the day, on the other hand, are *feminine*, because the word **hora** is feminine: **la hora**. There are four things that English-speaking students of Spanish need to keep in mind when dealing with the time of day.

First, all times of the day are expressed as plurals, except when the point of reference is one o'clock, morning or afternoon. Secondly, many students seem to have difficulty distinguishing between telling what the hour is and telling at what time something takes place. Examine the following examples of questions and answers:

¿Qué hora es?	*What time is it?*
Son **las cuatro** y veinte.	*It's four twenty.*

But:

Es **la una** menos cuarto.	*It's quarter to one.*
Es **la una** y media.	*It's one-thirty.*
¿A **qué hora** te acuestas?	*What time do you go to bed?*
Me acuesto a **las once** y media.	*I go to bed at eleven-thirty.*

With analog clocks and military time, used in some Latin American countries (most notably in Argentina), the following example shows how one displayed military time could be expressed verbally. In American military parlance, the word *hours* is often expressed as a singular in *casual* speech. Rapid speech in Spanish could also result in the suppression of the **y** or **con**:

---

* An alternate spelling of *September* in Spanish is **setiembre**.

| 13:25 | Son las trece (y/con) veinticinco horas | *Thirteen hundred (and) twenty-five hour(s)* |

Radio DJs, sports announcers, and others who work in live media are often creative with how they express the hour. The spontaneous variations are unpredictable and sometimes, just as in English, they can be mildly amusing. However, one will often hear the following, particularly when a new hour is drawing nigh:

| Son seis (minutos) pa'(ra) las cuatro de la tarde. | *It's six t' four in the afternoon.* |

The abbreviations A.M. and P.M. are used in print but, the letters are not spoken. (Spanish tends to avoid speaking acronyms.) Instead, as appropriate or needed for clarity, you can append the phrases **de la mañana** (*in the morning*), **de la tarde** (*in the afternoon*), and **de la noche** (*at night*). Also, don't forget the grammatical genders of *morning*, *afternoon*, and *night* so you can properly greet people:

| Buenos días, señor. | *Good morning, sir.* |

But:

| Buenas tardes/noches, señorita. | *Good afternoon/evening/night, Miss.* |

When reporting time in the past, just as when telling someone's age in the past, always use the imperfect:

Era la una.	*It was one.*
Eran las cinco de la tarde.	*It was five in the afternoon.*
Mi hermana mayor **tenía** cinco años cuando nací.	*My older sister was five years old when I was born.*

Finally, while the word for *season* is feminine (**la estación**), the individual seasons vary in grammatical gender. When speaking of seasons, the articles or demonstrative adjectives are used:

la primavera	*spring*
el verano	*summer*
el otoño	*fall*
el invierno	*winter*

En la primavera, espero viajar a San Francisco en tren.	*In the spring, I hope to travel to San Francisco by train.*
Ese otoño llovió mucho.	*It rained a lot that fall.*
Este verano, mis amigos van a Oregon.	*This summer, my friends are going to Oregon.*

Compare the formatting conventions for the printed form for recording the date. Note that in Spanish the date comes before the month (**lunes** is capitalized only because it is the first word in the line). The word **de** before the year can also be replaced by a comma:

| Lunes, 16 de enero de 2012 | *Monday, January 16, 2012* |

Compare how this date would be expressed in full sentences in English and Spanish, such as in the opening of a national news program on television or radio:

| Hoy es lunes, dieciséis de enero del año dos mil doce. | *Today is Monday, the sixteenth of January, two thousand twelve.* |

When speaking or writing of the first day in a month, the ordinal is used: **primero** (*first*), abbreviated as 1º. After the first of the month, the cardinal numbers are used to write and say the date:

Es el primero de mayo.	*It's May first.*
Mañana es el dos de mayo.	*Tomorrow is May second.*

On a form, such as a job application, the formula in English is *month/day/year*. In Spanish, it is *day/month/year*. Here's one way that the date could appear in a form in the Spanish-speaking world and in an American form (the abbreviations for the months are almost the same as in English, except for January):

16/ene/2012	01/16/2012

Most students learn that when verbally expressing address and phone numbers in Spanish, the number is broken into two-digit parts as much as possible. Where to break up an odd series seems to depend more on the relative ease of pronouncing the result. There is no hard-and-fast rule, but zeroes cause one or more numbers to be stated separately. Observe in the following that (206) 284–7960 in English becomes 2-0-6; 2-84; 79-60 in Spanish. Likewise, a number in an English address changes from 1608 Avenida Cuatro Oeste to 16-0-8 Avenida Cuatro Oeste.

EJERCICIO
19·1

Match the English words and phrases with their corresponding Spanish translations.

_____	1.	fall	a.	la temporada
_____	2.	season (of the year)	b.	el verano
_____	3.	January	c.	jueves
_____	4.	season (for a sport)	d.	la estación
_____	5.	winter	e.	sábado
_____	6.	On Mondays	f.	miércoles
_____	7.	On Friday	g.	el invierno
_____	8.	Saturday	h.	la primavera
_____	9.	Wednesday	i.	enero
_____	10.	spring	j.	los lunes
_____	11.	summer	k.	el viernes
_____	12.	Thursday	l.	el otoño

Write out how you would say the following sentences in Spanish that include numbers in addresses, telephone numbers, time of day, days of the week, and month and year.

1. On Saturday, March 12, 2011, I finished writing this book.

   _____

2. The soccer game began at 1:15 P.M. on Saturday, January 8, 2011.

   _____

3. Last year, March 1st was on a Monday.

   _____

4. By 4 P.M. today, I will have worked for ten hours.

   _____

5. On Monday, I have an appointment at 3 P.M.

   _____

6. What time did the movie begin?

   _____

7. He lived at 305 N. Eighth Street from June 1978 until August 1980.

   _____

8. Don't forget to call me some evening at 235–1102. (**tú**)

   _____

9. In Spanish-speaking countries, Tuesday, not Friday, the 13th is considered unlucky.

   _____

10. Do you know what happened on Friday, October 12, 1492? (**Ud.**)

    _____

11. The White House is at 1600 Pennsylvania Avenue.

    _____

12. I think her number is 247–9538, but don't call her on Sundays. (**Ud.**)

    _____

13. She was born on 01/22/98 at 9:44 A.M. It was a Thursday.

    _____

14. 11/22/63 was a Friday.

    _____

15. It's 12:01 A.M.

   _____

16. On Thursdays, I go to bed at 12:45 A.M., which means that on Wednesdays, I don't go to bed!

   _____

17. The library is on 4th Avenue. Beginning in March, it opens at 9 A.M. every day except Sundays.

   _____

18. It's 22:45 hrs.

   _____

19. (Write out your birthday, including as much information as you know).

   _____

20. (Write your phone number, dividing it into as many two-digit combinations as are easy to say).

   _____

Numbers, math, and statistics

This chapter will enable you to use and understand rudimentary arithmetical terminology. It covers vocabulary used to express social and economic data as found in non-specialist media or heard on television and radio. For readers who are experts in these fields, this chapter is a good primer to help them begin to express themselves in professional contexts.

Cardinal vs. ordinal numbers

Cardinal numbers are adjectives used to count (**uno**, **dos**, **tres**), but unlike other adjectives (except for **uno** in its role as an indefinite pronoun), they do not show gender—and they already show number! *Ordinal* numbers, as the name says, are adjectives. They are used to arrange things, people, ideas, and events into some sort of order, whether chronologically or in terms of importance (**primero**, **segundo**, **tercero**). Note that **primero** and **tercero** drop the final -**o** when they modify a singular masculine noun.

The ordinals (listed in their masculine form), *first* through *tenth* are:

primero	*first*
segundo	*second*
tercero	*third*
cuarto	*fourth*
quinto	*fifth*
sexto	*sixth*
séptimo	*seventh*
octavo	*eighth*
noveno	*ninth*
décimo	*tenth*

Like all quantifying adjectives, both cardinal and ordinal numbers precede the nouns they modify. Remember that Spanish avoids using ordinal numbers beyond the ordinal **décimo** (*tenth*). With dates however, only the *first* of the month is expressed as an ordinal. Observe the following examples:

Mis amigos fueron **los primeros** en volver de la excursión a la montaña.	*My friends were the first to return from the mountain tour.*
Según la leyenda de Génesis, Adán fue **el primer** hombre y Eva la primera mujer.	*According to the Genesis legend, Adam was the first man and Eve the first woman.*
Sus padres van a Caracas **el primero** de junio.	*Her parents are going to Caracas on June first.*

When using the cardinal numbers, the word **otros** must come before the number, whereas *other* can go either before or after the number in English. When an ordinal and a cardinal number modify the same noun, the cardinal comes first in Spanish—this time the reverse of English. Compare the following examples:

Vamos a entrevistar a **los otros tres** postulantes.	*Let's interview the other three (the three other) applicants.*
Los dos primeros platos que aprendí a preparar no eran difíciles.	*The first two dishes I learned to cook weren't difficult.*

Note how the meaning of the first example changes when **los** is omitted before **otros**:

Vamos a entrevistar a **otros tres** postulantes.	*Let's interview three more candidates.*

Fractions

In order to express fractions in Spanish, the cardinal numbers are used for the numerator. This is the same as English. For fractions beginning with 1/4 to 10/10, the cardinal numbers are used as denominators, except for *half*, which is called **medio** and *thirds*, which are **tercio(s)**.

un medio	1/2
un tercio	1/3
dos tercios	2/3
un cuarto	1/4
tres quintos	3/5
dos sextos	2/6
seis séptimos	6/7
tres octavos	3/8
cuatro novenos	4/9
cuatro décimos	4/10

Beginning with 1/11, numerators continue being cardinals, but the denominators are formed by adding the suffix -**avo** to the cardinal number. They can be a bit cumbersome to say; for example:

dos diecisieteavos	2/17
tres veinteavos	3/20

But:

un centavo (*not* cientavo)	1/100

There is a way to avoid these tongue-twisters (evidently even Spanish speakers need a way out). One can use the word **parte(s)** (*part[s]*), which is feminine, with the ordinal forms in the feminine, to agree with it. The only disadvantage is that this structure leaves unsaid the idea of "parts of *what* whole." Therefore, it is more common in cooking or when giving instructions for mixing diverse ingredients such as fertilizer:

las dos terceras partes	*two thirds*
tres quintas partes	*three fifths*

Finally, remember that as an adjective **medio** is *half* (and agrees with any noun it modifies) and **mitad** is the noun for *a half*:

Ella me vendió **media** docena de huevos.	*She sold me half a dozen eggs.*
El proyecto se atrasó **medio** mes por la lluvia.	*The project was half a month behind due to rain.*
Juan se comió **la mitad** de la torta.	*John gobbled up half the cake.*

Arithmetic operations

It's easy to verbalize the four basic arithmetic operations. You need to know the cardinal numbers and the verbs or expressions for the operations. The verb **ser** is less often used nowadays to express the result; the more common expression is **igual a** (*to [be] equal [to]*) or **equivale a** (used in the singular regardless of the number that follows). **Igual a** is particularly handy when expressing results involving *one* plus a fraction. Here are those verbs and expressions:

> más *or* y +
> dividido por (*or* entre) ÷
> es/son; igual a =
> menos –
> **[multiplicado] por** ×
> por ciento %

One aspect of recording and expressing numbers that can initially confuse English speakers is the fact that in many countries, comma and decimal usage is the reverse of US usage. Thus, 5.34 becomes 5,34 and 4,352.5 becomes 4.352,5. In countries where this is the case, when saying these numbers, you would say **coma** instead of **punto**:

Cinco coma treinta y cuatro	5,34
Cuatro mil, trescientos cincuenta y dos, coma cinco	4.352,5

The trickiest part for English speakers is no surprise—remembering to make the verbs agree in number with the numbers that are their subjects. Observe how the following operations are expressed:

Dos más dos son cuatro.	2 + 2 = 4
Trece menos cinco son ocho.	13 – 5 = 8
Noventa y nueve más uno son cien.	99 + 1 = 100
Cien menos noventa y nueve es uno.	100 – 99 = 1
Cinco (multiplicado) por cinco son veinticinco.	5 × 5 = 25
Setenta y tres dividido por/entre nueve son ocho, con dos restantes (*or* y quedan/ restan dos).	73 ÷ 9 = 8, r2

Percentages, rates, and fees

One common error is that of confusing the words **por ciento** (*percent*) and **el porcentaje** (*percentage*). The distinct usages are identical in both languages. One convention should be observed when writing or speaking of *percentages* expressed numerically as a *percent*: always use the indefinite article **el** in front of the number. Note that the article **el** also makes the verb **ser** singular, since the group of 5% is considered collectively: **El 5%** (expressed aloud as **el cinco por ciento**) **de la población es analfabeta.**

When the English word *rate* is used with the meaning of *index* or *frequency*, the usual Spanish word is **tasa**. When rate refers to a *fee* or other financial *charge*, it is **tarifa** or **cuota**. A *fine*, closely related in the transactional sense, is called **una multa**. The verb phrase for *to fine* is **poner(le) una multa**. When *rate* is used in the sense of *exchange rate*, the Spanish word is **el tipo de cambio**. For engineers, the word *rate* usually involves **la velocidad** (*velocity*) or **el volumen** (*volume*). Additionally, the concept of *per* is often expressed using **por**, but also by **el, al** or **la, a la**, depending on the type and gender of the unit of measurement. Observe the following examples:

La agencia tomó medidas para reducir **la tasa** de analfabetismo en la región.	*The agency took measures to lower the illiteracy rate in the region.*
Los aduaneros me cobraron **una tarifa** de 20 pesos **por** la importación de estos bienes.	*The customs officers charged me a 20 peso fee to import these goods.*
¿Cuánto es **la cuota** de ingreso para el gimnasio?	*How much is the membership (joining) fee for the health club?*
El policía le dio una multa de $50 **por** exceso de velocidad.	*The police gave him a $50 fine for speeding.*
¿Cuál es **el tipo de cambio** hoy?	*What is today's exchange rate?*
El volumen del derrame excedió **los** 2 millones de barriles al/por mes.	*The spill rate exceeded 2 million barrels per month.*
El petróleo salía del tubo de perforación a **una velocidad** de 50 kilómetros **la/por** hora.	*The gas was spilling from the bore tube at 50 km. per hour.*

Forms, charts, and graphs

In order to discuss what numbers actually mean, you need to know vocabulary related to their contexts. In other words, you need to know a handful of terms commonly used to refer to the types of documents, figures, and diagrams in which statistics and numbers are recorded. The English word for a *form*, as in something to fill out, is either **un formulario** or **una planilla**. The choice is mostly a regional preference. The little *boxes* that have to be filled in also can be called either **los encasillados** or **las casillas**.

The word for a *table* (as in a *diagram*) can be **un cuadro** or **una tabla**. As for how to express *graphics*, the choice depends on the design of the visual. For a *pie chart*, use **un gráfico de sectores**; for a *bar graph*, use **un gráfico de barras**. Keep in mind that in most of these common words or phrases, one choice is masculine, the other feminine, so be prepared if you need to use a direct object pronoun or other pronominal forms to refer to them.

La planilla? Ah, la puse ahí.	*The form? Oh, I put it there.*
Entre **los cuadros** a continuación, quiero llamar su atención a éste.	*Among the following tables, I wish to draw your attention to this one.*

Statistics

Among the many statistical terms, *range* is one of the most frequently encountered. The best translations for this concept that will work in nearly every use, except golf and ballistics, is **la gama** (the *spread*, as in from one point through others to an end point) or **el abanico** (literally, *fan*, like the ones found in Asia). These two terms also have a close affinity to **la variabilidad** (*variability*), although they are not synonymous.

The term *standard deviation* is **la desviación normal** (or **estándar**). Other words any statistician or responsible citizen will need include **el promedio** (*average*), **la mediana** (*median*), **el valor medio** (*mean*), **el modo** (mode), **el eje-x** and **el eje-y** (*x*- and *y*-axis), and of course **máximo/mínimo** (*minimum/maximum*) and **límite superior/inferior** (*upper/lower limit*). These are probably all the terms anyone would need to know (and understand) in order to talk about news items written and broadcast for the general public.

Según este gráfico, **el valor medio** es 45.	*According to this graph, the median is 45.*
El límite superior en la prueba fue de 300 partes por millón.	*The upper limit in the test was 300 parts per million.*

The stock market

Let's start with that: **La Bolsa de Valores**. Beyond that, it is important to realize that the English world's lingo of high finance is colorful in the extreme. In it you can find animals: *bears* and *bulls*, and acronyms that spell or are pronounced as animal names: *TIGR*, comes to mind. The Spanish-speaking world of high finance, when it is not borrowing freely from English, is drab and matter-of-fact by comparison. This is because Spanish tends to focus on verbs—the action—while English focuses on nouns.

Thus a *bear market* is said to be **un mercado de tendencia bajista** (from the verb **bajar**, *to go down*), while a *bull market* is **un mercado de tendencia alcista** (from the verb **alzar**, *to rise*). Likewise, one hears and reads of **el alza** or **la baja del mercado** (*the rising* or *the falling of the market*). **Stock brokers** are called **corredores de acciones** or **corredores de valores** (from the verb **correr**—because they do a lot of running, figuratively and literally).

Options are, well, **opciones**. In Spanish, *a put option* is called by a name that almost makes it understandable to non-brokers: **una opción a vender**. The same is true of *a call option*, which is **una opción a comprar**. As is true in any business, *the profits* are **las ganancias** or **los beneficios** and *the margin* is **el margen**. Armed with these terms, a good ear, and a decent general verb vocabulary, you should be able to read the financial section of the newspaper with relative confidence.

El inversionista se puso nervioso a causa del **mercado de tendencia bajista**.	*The investor got nervous because of the bear market.*
Algunos vieron la tendencia bajista y decidieron comprar **una opción a vender**.	*Some saw the downward trend and decided to buy a put action.*

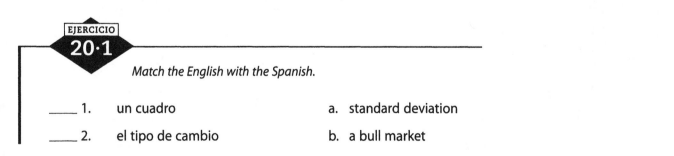

EJERCICIO
20·1

Match the English with the Spanish.

_____ 1.   un cuadro   a.   standard deviation

_____ 2.   el tipo de cambio   b.   a bull market

_____ 3.	la bolsa de valores	c.	average
_____ 4.	la tasa	d.	form
_____ 5.	una opción a vender	e.	margin
_____ 6.	un gráfico de sectores	f.	percent
_____ 7.	el porcentaje	g.	the spread/range
_____ 8.	un mercado de tendencia alcista	h.	index/frequency
_____ 9.	el eje-_x_	i.	divided by
_____ 10.	la desviación normal	j.	variability
_____ 11.	un formulario	k.	table
_____ 12.	dividido por	l.	percentage
_____ 13.	el por ciento	m.	a call option
_____ 14.	el promedio	n.	upper limit
_____ 15.	por año	o.	pie chart
_____ 16.	el margen	p.	mean
_____ 17.	el valor medio	q.	stock market
_____ 18.	la variabilidad	r.	_x_-axis
_____ 19.	límite superior	s.	exchange rate
_____ 20.	el abanico	t.	per annum

EJERCICIO
20·2

Write out how you would express aloud the following basic mathematical operations and express the following values.

1. 3 + 5 = 8 _____

2. 42 × 34 = 1,428 _____

3. 89 ÷ 7 = 12, r5 _____

4. 77 − 52 = 25 _____

5. 93 × 7 = 651 _____

6. 2/3 _____

7. 2/7 _____

8. 3/4 _____

9. 1/2 _____

10. 4/5 _____

11. 3/4 + 1/2 = 1 1/4 _____

12. 5,3 − 4,1 = 1,2 _____

13. 6 − 5 = 1 _____

14. 97% _____

15. 101 − 1 = 100 _____

16. 10 × 100 = 1000 _____

17. 1000 + 1 = 1001 _____

18. 777 + 555 = 1,332 _____

19. 3/7 _____

20. 23% _____

Translate the following sentences from Spanish to English.

1. Se cree que la tendencia bajista de la bolsa seguirá a menos que la Reserva tome medidas.

   _____

2. Se ha calculado que la tasa de mortalidad por la peste bubónica fue del 30% de la población.

   _____

3. La secretaria me mostró un panfleto con un gráfico de barras.

   _____

4. El corredor de valores tiene una opción a comprar que caduca a la hora del cierre de operaciones.

   _____

5. La tasa de crecimiento de la economía se ha disminuido debido a las guerras civiles en la región.

   _____

6. La cuota de ingreso es $187 y desde entonces es $140 al año.

   _____

7. La junta de directores anunció que reinvertirá el 5% de las ganancias en campañas publicitarias.

   _____

8. La cantidad dedicada a la educación es el 4% menos este año con respecto al año pasado.

_____

9. Un estudio de las condiciones económicas reveló que hay un abanico de posibilidades para resolver la crisis.

_____

10. Los acreedores han propuesto un aumento del 4% en el tipo de interés.

_____

11. Por una semana, el precio del valor vaciló entre $40 y $50.

_____

12. El Congreso aprobó un aumento del 2% para los bienes de consumo importados.

_____

13. Para poner de manifiesto su oposición a la postura anti-sindicalista del gobernador, los obreros salieron en huelga.

_____

_____

14. El personal a cargo de investigación y desarrollo recibió un aumento de sueldo del 4%.

_____

15. Debido a que la tasa de inflación está al 9% al año y a que la del desempleo se acerca al 12%, es dudoso que en las próximas elecciones el partido en el poder vaya a permanecer en control ni de los cuerpos legislativos ni de los puestos ejecutivos.

_____

_____

_____

Answer key

1 Spelling and pronunciation

1·1 *The stressed vowels are underlined.*   1. missing; organiza<u>ció</u>n   2. missing; c<u>ó</u>nsul
3. correct, no accent mark; le<u>a</u>ltad   4. superfluous; anim<u>al</u>   5. correctly used; cami<u>ó</u>n
6. missing; tecnolog<u>í</u>a   7. sup<u>e</u>rfluous; h<u>a</u>blas   8. missing; te<u>ó</u>rico   9. correct, no
accent mark; temer<u>a</u>ria   10. correct, no accent mark; primor<u>o</u>sa   11. missing; car<u>á</u>cter
12. incorrectly placed; avi<u>ó</u>n   13. correct, no accent mark; caract<u>e</u>res   14. missing;
vendi<u>ó</u>   15. superfluous; vent<u>a</u>na   16. correct, no accent mark; vec<u>i</u>no   17. correct,
no accent mark; frij<u>o</u>les (Note: in Colombia: **frí<u>j</u>oles**)   18. correct, no accent mark;
proyect<u>o</u>r   19. correct, no accent mark; cort<u>i</u>nas   20. correctly used; teor<u>í</u>a

2 Forms of address, statements and questions, and social conventions

2·1   1. Ud.   2. tú   3. tú   4. Ud.   5. vosotros   6. Uds.   7. vosotros   8. Uds.
9. tú   10. vosotras

2·2   1. b   2. a   3. b   4. a   5. b   6. c   7. b   8. a   9. a   10. b   11. b
12. b   13. a   14. a   15. a

3 Articles

3·1   1. unas   2. los   3. (*no article is used before* **mil**)   4. (*no article is used before titles in
direct address*)   5. los   6. un   7. unos   8. el   9. (*no article is used before* **otro**)
10. los   11. los (*unless they are lionesses, then* **las**)   12. el (*if female, the abbreviation
would be* **Dra.**, *and thus the article would be* **la**)   13. unos   14. las   15. la; el

3·2   1. b   2. b   3. a   4. c   5. a   6. b   7. c   8. b   9. c   10. c (*option a singles
Paulina out from a group and identifies her as the one who is Spanish; option b states that
she is a Spaniard. Only option c simply says that she's Spanish*)   11. b (*option a omits*
todos; *option c omits* **todos** *and uses the passive voice, not the best choice in Spanish*)
12. b   13. b   14. c (*options a and b wrongly assume knowledge of her marital status; c
uses* **dama**, *a better term for* lady)   15. a

4 Gender and number agreement

4·1   1. el tercer edificio   2. el pobre niño   3. los cinco primeros ganadores   4. el primer
coche   5. media hora (*the article* **una** *is not used*)   6. la francesa alta   7. el único
gato   8. los perros grandes   9. el último libro   10. mi propia mochila   11. el
amarillo sol   12. mi antigua novia   13. las nueve manzanas rojas   14. unos niños
pobres   15. unas casas muy bonitas   16. un cuento fascinante / una historia
fascinante   17. unas noches largas   18. un viejo / anciano raro   19. el gran héroe
20. la primera niña / muchacha

4·2   1. b   2. b   3. b (*the use of* **varias** *and* **niñitas** *makes this a better choice than* c)
4. a   5. b (*the position of* **alguno** *stresses the expected negative response*)   6. b
7. b (a *expresses probability in the present by using the future;* c *expresses wonder. Only* b *expresses the notion of some backpack somewhere around here*)   8. b   9. b (a *and* c *place the adjective in the wrong place for expressing that the house was previously owned and instead assert that it was newly built*)   10. b   11. b
12. a (b *is wrong because of the placement of the adjective* **cierta**; c *is wrong because* **una** *is not used before* **cierta**)   13. b (*the only option that expresses the idea that* single *conveys in English*)   14. b   15. c

5   Demonstrative adjectives, demonstrative pronouns, and neuter pronouns

5·1   1. estas dos alumnas   2. este sombrero   3. esta primera montaña   4. esos cuadros / esas pinturas
5. aquella luz   6. este museo   7. esos libros antiguos / viejos   8. este espejo antiguo   9. aquella caja de libros   10. este perro amable   11. esta camisa roja   12. esa mujer delgada   13. esa clase
14. estos vestidos bonitos   15. estos zapatos pardos   16. esos jugadores de fútbol (*or* esas jugadoras de fútbol)   17. aquel hombre   18. aquel barco de vela   19. estos seis carros nuevos   20. esta casa antigua

5·2   1. a   2. b   3. b (*the placement of* **ese** *makes it the best choice*)   4. b (*the placement of* esa *makes it the best choice*)   5. b   6. b (**aquella** *conveys remoteness while* **época** *expresses a time period*)   7. b (**señor**, *in option* a, *is too formal as a translation for* guy, *while the position of* **grande** *in option* c *makes its meaning literal*)   8. a (b *assumes too much, i.e., that something has to be accomplished after studying the subject*)
9. c.   10. a   11. b   12. c (**decir** *expresses the idea of telling something to others, while* **lo de ayer** *expresses* that business about)   13. b   14. a   15. a

6   Reflexive pronouns

6·1   1. q   2. s   3. t   4. o   5. i   6. l   7. b   8. r   9. n   10. c   11. d   12. p   13. g
14. j   15. k   16. h   17. a   18. e   19. f   20. m

6·2   1. Do you know if there's an apartment for rent in this building?   2. John and Mary took off running when they heard the bomb blast.   3. Nothing was heard for several hours after the incident.
4. My homework? The dog ate it. (*the English possessive achieves what* **me** *does in Spanish*)   5. Geez! Just take the medicine already / and be done with it!   6. A friend of mine gave me this antique ring as a gift.
7. Mr. Martinez got up, took the proposal from the table, and took it with him.   8. You told them that? But, man—it was a secret!   9. Our car broke down on the road and we had to call my uncle.   10. The postcard? I sent it to our parents yesterday.   11. How do you make a salad, Mom? (*you, as in one:* how does one *or even* how is a salad prepared?)   12. The gift is for you. I went with my brother to buy it for you.
13. The boss needs the hammer. So, loan it to him then.   14. The mechanic's hands are dirty. He's going to wash them before using the phone.   15. What do I do day in and day out? Well, nothing less than what you / one has to do.   16. Thomas's bill? I'm preparing it for him now.   17. Do you want to see that movie with me or with him?   18. The couple was looking at each other all the time.   19. That guy seems crazy—he talks to himself all the time.   20. Mr. Acero doesn't get embarrassed even when his lies are exposed.

6·3   1. ¿Cómo se parara una buena ensalada?   2. El bebé se cayó.   3. Se rompió el plato.   4. Ella se puso un par de zapatos nuevos.   5. El perro se lamió las patas.   6. Se recuperó / se mejoró rápidamente.
7. ¡Subieron / escalaron la montaña inmediatamente / en seguida / directamente / sin demora!
8. El sweater se deshizo antes de que ella pudiera terminar de tejerlo.   9. Se prometieron amarse.
10. Nos buscábamos el uno al otro todo el día.   11. Se los dimos (a ellos).   12. Llegaron a ser / se hicieron maestros.   13. Ella se peinó y se puso maquillaje.   14. Se lo vendí (a ellos).   15. Se colgó la camisa en una percha.   16. Ella se alegró de que la hubieras llamado.   17. En Macondo, no se pintaron las casas de rojo.   18. Él se asustó con el ruido / El ruido lo asustó.   19. Se escribió esta carta en el siglo diecinueve.   20. Se colgaron las medias con cuidado junto a la chimenea.

6·4   1. Él se miró en el espejo ayer.   2. Ellos se compraron regalos anoche.   3. Los zapatos se perdieron esta mañana en la playa.   4. Anoche el vino se derramó en la mesa.   5. Ese día las campanas se repicaban para celebrar la paz.   6. El Sr. Acero se condenará pronto.   7. Ellas se creían lo máximo.
8. Los niños se durmieron a las ocho ayer.   9. Ella se levanta a las siete de la mañana.   10. Ellos se enojaron de que tú no hicieras / no hubieras hecho la tarea ayer.   11. El bebé se toma / se está tomando /

está tomándose la leche ahora.   12. Juan y María se abrazaron anoche en el parque.   13. Mientras ella se vestía anoche, ellos se durmieron en el sofá.   14. Anoche, se la escribí.   15. Juan se enojó al irse.   16. Hansel no se perdía en el / bosque nunca.   17. La mantequilla se derrite si no se pone en la nevera.   18. Se perdió el juicio Don Quijote.   19. ¿Cómo se escribe / su nombre?   20. Él fue a esquiar ayer y se le rompió la pierna.

7   Double object pronouns

7·1   1. t   2. i   3. g   4. j   5. k   6. a.   7. l   8. b   9. m   10. f   11. c   12. d   13. r   14. s   15. e   16. n   17. o   18. h   19. p   20. q

7·2   1. Ella le lava las manos de él.   2. Se lo queremos comprar / Queremos comprárselo.   3. ¡Tráemelo!   4. Ella esperaba encontrárselos.   5. ¡No me la mandes / envíes!   6. Él debe grabárselas.   7. Me los dan / Me los están dando / Están dándomelos.   8. Nos lo dio para la Navidad.   9. Se la mandaron ayer.   10. Se la mandará / Se la va a mandar / Va a mandársela *(or, with* **enviar***)*.   11. Queremos hacérsela / Se la queremos hacer.   12. Ella no quería tejérselo / no se lo quería tejer. (**no quiso** *would mean* she refused).   13. Nos los trajeron.   14. Ella se la preparó.   15. Queremos comprártelo / Te lo queremos comprar.   16. Ellos están construyéndosela / Ellos se la están construyendo.   17. ¡No me la compres!   18. Se lo debo dar / Debo dárselo.   19. ¿Quieres mandársela? / ¿Se la quieres mandar?   20. No se la vamos a mandar / No vamos a mandársela.

7·3   1. Tú se los quieres mandar / Tú quieres mandárselos ahora.   2. Yo se la tuve que comprar anoche / Yo tuve que comprársela anoche.   3. Se lo íbamos a vender la semana pasada. / Íbamos a vendérselo la semana pasada.   4. Ellos no se la deben servir. / Ellos no deben servírsela.   5. Tú se lo estás escribiendo en este momento. / Tú estás escribiéndoselo en este momento.   6. ¡Arréglanosla!   7. Él me lo trajo ayer.   8. Yo se la voy a poner pronto. / Voy a ponérsela pronto.   9. Ella me la hizo esta mañana.   10. Uds. se los querían dar el fin de semana pasado. / Ellos querían dárselos el fin de semana pasado.   11. Los niños me la rompieron el domingo pasado.   12. Ella se lo va a pedir mañana. / Ella va a pedírselo mañana.   13. ¡No se la manden!   14. Nosotros no te lo podemos mandar ahora. / Nosotros no podemos mandártelo ahora.   15. Ella se lo quería dar anoche. / Ella quería dárselo anoche. (**quiso** *means* she tried).   16. Tú nos la debes mostrar ahora. / Tú debes mostrárnosla ahora.   17. ¡Déselo!   18. Yo se los quería pedir. / Yo quería pedírselos. (**quise** *means* I tried.)   19. Ella se las va a enviar esta tarde. / Ella va a enviárselas esta tarde.   20. Él se la quería escribir la semana pasada. / Él quería escribírsela la semana pasada.(**Quiso** *means* he tried.)

8   Prepositions and translating English phrasal verbs

8·1   1. o   2. i   3. d   4. r   5. l   6. a   7. c   8. n   9. e   10. s   11. t   12. g   13. j   14. h   15. b   16. m.   17. k   18. f   19. q   20. p

8·2   1. m   2. n   3. j   4. r   5. h   6. b   7. p   8. c   9. k   10. t   11. d   12. s   13. e   14. a   15. g   16. f   17. i   18. l   19. q   20. o

8·3   1. por *(exchange)*   2. por *(along; across)*   3. por *(per)*   4. por *(object of errand)*   5. Para *(purpose, refers to* **a pintar***)* or Por *(cause:* **por eso** *= for that reason)*   6. por *(for the sake of)*   7. para *(purpose:* **para colmo** *= to top it off)*   8. Por *(why)*   9. para *(direction)*   10. para *(recipient)*   11. por *(in place of)*   12. por *(around here)*   13. para *(deadline)*   14. para *(purpose: in order to)*   15. para *(purpose: in order to)*   16. Para *(purpose)*   17. Por *(cause)*   18. por *(for that reason)*   19. para *(purpose: in order to)*   20. por *(around;* **para** *would indicate they spent an hour walking toward the park)*

8·4   1. That family went through the town / village in March every year.   2. The war hero nearly gave his life for the freedom of his country. (**Por poco** *is an idiomatic expression used with verbs in the present, but its meaning is past).*   3. Due to his limited notions about politics, I tried to convince him with mine.   4. The water flowed over a bed of rocks between two mountains.   5. The hamlet was founded on the banks of the river.   6. A man fell through the roof when he tried to rob the house.   7. The old woman with curly hair buried a figurine full of gold under the bed.   8. Wherever he / she went, soft music could be / was heard.   9. The younger brother, by effort and talent, worked for years to fix up the house.   10. It rained for several days.   11. A man got on / boarded the train that was going nowhere, without any particular route and no destination.   12. The woman who lives on the floor below was the only one who felt pity for him / her.   13. The dogs ran after the rabbit.   14. The overland / mule-train mail route ran / passed through the mountains.   15. The musician was sitting in the middle of / surrounded by the disassembled pieces of a harpsichord.   16. The doves, frightened by the woman's cry, flew up toward the clouds.   17. Due to his insanity, several men had to restrain him with ropes / cords.   18. The spear the hero hurled flew until it pierced the chest of the enemy general.   19. The accused had to appear before the judge.   20. The city sank in the mud.

8·5   1. Por poco el perro corrió debajo del autobús.   2. La casa está / queda / se ubica / dentro de cinco millas de la ciudad.   3. El Sr. Acero no sólo hizo acusaciones sin evidencia, sino contra ella.   4. No nos dijo nada al respecto / sobre eso.   5. Ella se enojó con él cuando él entró en la casa.   6. Cuando salí del cine, vi a la muchacha de quien me había enamorado.   7. Ella me dijo que soñó conmigo.   8. No sabían si deberían casarse o no.   9. Resultó ser falsa la historia, según la cual él era de Italia.   10. Los niños corrieron por la casa, enlodando toda la alfombra.   11. ¡No traicione al rey, so pena de la muerte!   12. Buscaron hasta que encontraron todo lo que querían vender.   13. Por mi parte, dame la Libertad o la Muerte.   14. A pesar de sus diferencias, convinieron en firmar el tratado.   15. ¿De quién es este libro? (**¿Cuyo libro es?** *is admissible, but archaic.*)   16. En vez de quejarte, debes trabajar.   17. La biblioteca está cerca del edificio en que trabajo.   18. ¿Espera ella hablar con él?   19. A pesar de lo que ella dijo, él le interesa a ella.   20. Marcharon por el desierto.

9   The preterit and imperfect tenses

9·1   1. miraba   2. comías   3. tenía   4. veía   5. habíamos   6. hacían   7. trabájabais   8. quería   9. podían   10. debían   11. era   12. veía   13. ibas   14. podía   15. era   16. iba   17. establecían   18. leíamos   19. escribía   20. creías

9·2   1. vi   2. sentiste   3. supo   4. cupieron   5. di   6. viajó   7. vivieron   8. traje   9. trabajamos (*the* **nosotros** *form of* **-ar** *verbs is the same in present indicative and preterit*)   10. quiso   11. entretuve (*compounds of irregular verbs are irregular in the same pattern*)   12. condujiste   13. tuve   14. hubisteis   15. hablaron   16. puse   17. estuvo   18. comiste   19. pudieron   20. hiciste

9·3   1. While my sisters were talking, I was playing the guitar.   2. When *Star Wars* came out, I was 22 years old.   3. There were several men on the corner when the car skidded and crashed into the wall.   4. When we were on vacation, my friends and I would go skiing and to restaurants.   5. Where were you and what were you doing when the total eclipse of the sun happened?   6. We ate, rested, and watched TV for a while, then decided to go to the beach.   7. I didn't like it that the phone rang while I was fixing dinner.   8. The children were playing on the porch / patio when their grandmother arrived.   9. Elena was waking up when her father called.   10. It was four in the afternoon and raining when I left the movie theater.   11. My sister was four years old when I was born.   12. What was the weather like while you were going to the lake to ski?   13. My parents moved into another house when I was two years old.   14. The dog took off running after the rabbit as soon as he saw it.   15. At three o'clock sharp, I was waiting at the library entrance.   16. When it quit raining, we went back to the tent.   17. The dinner turned out well and the food was delicious.   18. That year, it snowed a lot in the city.   19. When I realized (that) I didn't have Web access, I decided to take off / leave / get out of there.   20. The band was playing and the people were dancing, but I felt alone.

9·4   1. Cuando llegué, el perro dormía / estaba dormido / estaba durmiendo.   2. Mientras comías, nuestro hermano trabajaba.   3. Ella salió / se fue cuando él llegó.   4. Alexandra tenía tres años cuando nos mudamos a Seattle.   5. Después de que subimos al taxi, empezó a llover.   6. Ayer fue un día muy frío para Seattle. (*the day is considered as a completed time period, hence preterit;* **día** *is masculine.*)   7. Él arreglaba la mesa cuando se lastimó la mano. (*don't use possessive with parts of the body*)   8. ¿Quisiste llamarme ayer?   9. Eran las cinco de la tarde, y llovía, cuando mis amigos decidieron visitarme.   10. Yo preparaba el rosbif mientras escribía este ejercicio.   11. Cuando yo ponía la mesa, mi amigo estaba abajo haciendo las maletas para su viaje.   12. Tres pájaros se posaban / estaban posados en un alambre cuando, de repente, el gato quiso subir para comerse uno.   13. Su mamá se sentó cuando oyó las noticias.   14. El Sr. Acero chismeaba, todos le escuchaban, pero sólo unos pocos le creían.   15. Quería acostarse pero tenía demasiado trabajo a entregar el día siguiente.   16. El avión aterrizó mientras nevaba.   17. Cuando paró el tren, los pasajeros bajaron.   18. Mientras el buque entraba en el puerto, los aduaneros lo detuvieron.   19. Mientras mi abuela tejía a punto de aguja, nosotros y el perro jugábamos.   20. Sus amigos de ella le trajo / llevó el regalo mientras ella almorzaba / comía el almuerzo.

9·5   1. eran   2. vivía   3. aceptó   4. exigió   5. sabía   6. pareció   7. aceptó   8. se preparaban   9. hacían   10. empacaban   11. llegaron   12. se alegraron   13. Llegó   14. Llovía   15. Salió

(**Salía** *is acceptable if the idea is* while they were on their way out.)   16. estaban   17. iban   18. Eran
19. abordaron   20. tuvieron   21. aterrizó   22. bajaron   23. se sorprendieron   24. hacía
25. estaban 26. era

10   Confusing verb pairs

10·1   1. h   2. i   3. e   4. m   5. j   6. f   7. l   8. d   9. k   10. a   11. c   12. b   13. g

10·2   1. One / You can tell by his good manners that he has been raised well.   2. My Russian friend knows a lot about physics and astronomy.   3. That book was printed in Barcelona.   4. "I am a sincere man, from where the palm trees grow." (*José Martí*)   5. My fishing rod has broken.   6. Where and when did your parents meet?   7. The french fries were fried a few minutes ago.   8. The shopping center isn't exactly in the center of the city.   9. The cars have been manufactured with great care.   10. I knew Adele well in high school but then we lost touch.   11. At this moment, I am sitting in front of my computer, writing this.
12. I have a letter written for the boss.   13. In Mexico, corn has been grown / cultivated for thousands of years / since thousands of years ago.   14. The cat didn't move from his spot for two hours, since he was expecting the mouse to come out.   15. Are you okay, guy? You look worried / preoccupied.   16. My daughter was three years old when we moved to Seattle.   17. The party was in Juliet's house and it was fantastic.   18. The little boy still hadn't put on his jacket when he left for school.   19. Help me move the sofa, please.   20. The store will be open until around nine.

10·3   1. Dejamos el carro en casa.   2. El pájaro estaba / estuvo empetrolado / cubierto de brea.   3. Dicho y hecho.   4. Él estaba casado pero su hermana siempre ha sido soltera.   5. Sus padres de ella no le dejan mirar la tele / no dejan que mire la tele.   6. ¿Conoces bien a María? (*note the use of the personal* **a**)
7. Estarán dormidos / durmiendo por un par de horas.   8. Él es cansado.   9. José es mexicano.
10. Este vestido es de seda.   11. La fiesta es en la playa. (*Events use* **ser**, *not* **estar**.)   12. Cuando salió, no dejó / abandonó sus memorias.   13. Éste es el carro de mi papá.   14. Él sabía la letra de docenas de canciones.   15. ¿Están cansados?   16. Julio César está muerto.   17. Nos conocimos en 1990.
18. Ella ha devuelto el libro.   19. El criminal confeso ha dicho la verdad.   20. Acabas de hacer este ejercicio. (**acabar** *contains the idea of* finishing, *so there is no need to use* **terminar**).

11   Using verbs to show politeness

11·1   1. debiera   2. puedes   3. querría   4. quisiéramos   5. pudiera   6. deberían   7. podría
8. debieras   9. puedo   10. debería   11. quiere   12. querríais

11·2   1. John ought not / shouldn't drive so fast.   2. Could you please help me with this suitcase?   3. I think she'd like very much to go out with John.   4. Well, you *should / ought to* go to the dance.   5. Could you kindly wait until we arrive / get there?   6. I would like to try this dessert.   7. Can you give me a hand with this job / task / homework?   8. It's obvious: she should quit smoking.   9. As much as we'd really like to loan you / him / her the money, we don't have that much.   10. Do you want to buy the salad if I buy the meat?   11. If you / they truly want to learn the lesson, you / they should / ought to turn off the TV.
12. It's true / certain (that) I want to do the homework, but I don't have time right now.   13. They really, truly would like to contribute more to the organization.   14. My brothers (and sisters) could / would be able to help you tomorrow.   15. Could you so kindly ask him to come to the meeting?   16. Johnny, you really, really shouldn't quit taking / going to your music lessons.   17. My (female) cousins want to drive now.   18. With gusto / much pleasure / most gladly we could support you in your campaign!
19. I know what I should / ought to do; it's a question of not losing heart / becoming discouraged.
20. Can you send us the tools within a couple of days?

11·3   1. Yo quisiera acompañarte, pero no puedo.   2. Ella debería llevar a su amigo/a.   3. Debemos leer más.
4. ¿Puedes ayudarme a preparar la cena?   5. Sus amigos pudieran hacer más para él.
6. Deben haberme devuelto la llave correcta.   7. Quisiéramos ir contigo al cine.   8. Ella quiere invitar a Juan a la fiesta.   9. Ellos quisieran llevar su perro.   10. Mi hermana debería practicar el violín más.
11. ¿Pudieran apagar la radio?   12. Ella y Ana debieran agradecerle a su mamá.   13. Él querría prestarle el dinero si se lo puede reembolsar pronto / con tal de que se lo pueda reembolsar pronto.   14. Su amigo debería dejar de fumar.   15. ¿Podrías traerme la silla?   16. Tú y tus amigos, ¿no quisieran ir a la playa?
17. Ella vendría, pero no puede.   18. Él y yo debemos arreglar el coche.   19. Ud. debería asistir a la escuela.   20. Yo quisiera invitarte a almorzar.

12 Translating *ago* with **hacer** clauses

12·1   1. c   2. c   3. c   4. b   5. b   6. b   7. b   8. a   9. b   10. b   11. c   12. b   13. b
14. a   15. c   16. b   17. c   18. a   19. a   20. b

12·2   1. Te preguntas qué nota sacaste en el último examen.   2. Ahora hace dos horas que ellos corren en el parque.   3. Hacía dos años que él jugaba al fútbol cuando se rompió la pierna.   4. Ayer a las tres yo estuve en la biblioteca, ¿dónde estaría Juan?   5. ¿Cuántos años hacía que tú conocías a tu novia cuando se casaron?   6. Hace una hora que yo comí.   7. No te sorprende que María y Juan se casen / se hayan casado / se casaran / se hubieran casado.   8. Le gustaría que ellos le acompañaran al cine.   9. Ayer ellos esperaban que tú llegaras, pero no llegaste. ¿Dónde estarías? (**estabas** *is used to ask a direct question, expecting an answer;* **estarías** *is used if the questioner is just wondering*)   10. ¿Quién sabe dónde estarán las llaves ahora / ? Él las pierde todo el tiempo.

12·3   1. We moved to this town a couple of years ago, when my daughter was three years old.   2. It didn't surprise him / He wasn't surprised that his brother won the race, since he had been training for a year.
3. Let's see / I wonder if there isn't a check in my mailbox.   4. No wonder Mr. Acero has been arrested—he's been cheating the employees for years.   5. John was wondering why María had not been answering him when he called her.   6. My parents had been living there for years.   7. How long has it been since you haven't / that you haven't seen your parents?   8. I exercised a lot an hour ago.   9. How long was Teresa setting the table? I wonder if she doesn't get distracted a lot.   10. We'd be very pleased if you would kindly return the book we loaned you a week ago.   11. How long ago did the tailor mend your overcoat?
12. The mechanic had been putting off the car inspection for some time. (**tardar** *can also mean* to take a long time doing something)   13. When / By the time (that) they arrested Mr. Acero, the authorities had been watching him for months.   14. Three weeks ago, five of my friends and I were witnesses to a paranormal event.   15. It lasted only a minute or less, but it seemed to us (that) we had been watching it for an hour.   16. We had been practicing for an hour when George made the lights go out.   17. I wonder if my friend has left a voice message for John.   18. When their window was broken a month ago, they didn't know / weren't sure if they should call the police.   19. Let's see / I wonder if my father hasn't called me.   20. I wonder what would have happened to me if I had not married her.

12·4   1. Quién sabe cómo él consiguió ese trabajo hace un año.   2. Ella se preguntaba si él le llamaría o no.
3. Hacía una hora que trabajaban cuando entró el jefe.   4. Hacía años que el Sr. Acero no decía la verdad.
5. Cuando terminó el drama, ella se dio cuenta de que hacía veinte minutos que dormía / estaba dormida.
6. Hacía un mes que él intentaba pedirle prestado dinero a su hermano.   7. Hace un año que somos los dueños del negocio.   8. Las flores se secaron porque hacía una semana que no las regaba.   9. Hace tres horas que duerme el perro.   10. Hacía cuatro años que yo vivía en Mazatlán cuando decidí volver a los EE. UU.   11. Hacía veinte minutos que se horneaba el pan cuando se apagó la luz. (**Luz** *is often used generically to refer to electric power.*)   12. Hace cerca de seis meses que su primo fue a Europa por dos semanas.   13. ¿Hace cuántos años que nació su abuelo?   14. ¿Cuánto tiempo hacía que ibas de compras cuando te diste cuenta de que habías perdido la tarjeta de crédito?   15. Hacía sólo diez minutos que se colgaba la ropa para secarla cuando empezó a llover.   16. Hace dos horas que ella estudia en su cuarto.
17. Cuando el submarino volvió a la superficie, hacía más de dos meses que estaba debajo del casquete glaciar polar.   18. Hace una hora por lo menos / cuando menos que él ronca en la mecedora.
19. Lo despertamos después de que hacía dos horas que dormía.   20. Con razón / No me extraña / sorprende que estés cansado/a: ¡estas oraciones son difíciles!

13 The **gustar** verb family

13·1   1. Geometry fascinates me but I don't like to study statistics.   2. My parents didn't (used to) like it at all when I got into mischief at school.   3. What do you say (*literally*: what does it seem like to you) if we go to Cancún for vacation?   4. This morning, my head hurt / was hurting until I took an aspirin.   5. When I met her, I told my friends right away how much she enchanted me.   6. Are you interested in studying with me?   7. It didn't matter to that guy if his sister didn't feel good.   8. I hope my readers like these exercises. (*Literally*: I hope these exercises please my readers.)   9. Jane had a headache but her stomach didn't hurt.   10. I know that if you went to Spain, you'd love *tapas*.   11. As a boy, watching insects was fascinating to him.   12. I've never liked that Mr. Acero.   13. It seemed odd that the little girl didn't like anything at school.   14. Before, I was interested in literature, but now I'm drawn to history and biographies.   15. I impress the young man with what I know about local history.   16. Politics doesn't matter to you? Well, perhaps it's because we don't matter much to the politicians.   17. Mary, I know (that) Henry likes you.   18. My (female) friend is fascinated by carnivorous plants. (*or* Carnivorous plants fascinate my friend.) 19. Aren't you repulsed by the smell of tobacco smoke? 20. My ears hurt when I listen to that woman sing.

13·2 1. Me gustas. 2. ¿Le gusto a ella? 3. ¿Os fascina la música clásica? 4. ¿No te parece raro su manera de escribir? 5. Creo que te gusto. 6. Antes les gustaba jugar al ajedrez, pero ya no. 7. Después de que ella dejó de fumar, aumentó de peso. 8. No les gustan. 9. ¿No les repugnan las películas violentas? 10. Después de que él volvió de la guerra, parecía que ni el dinero ni el poder le importaban. 11. Nos gusta mucho / encanta hacer helado. 12. (A él,) la sonrisa de ella le encantó / encantaba. 13. Sr. Acero, no me impresionas. 14. Me duele el pie. 15. ¿Qué cosa en la vida más te importa, Alexandra? 16. Le dolían las manos a su mamá. 17. A él le pareció raro que te gustaran los espárragos. 18. ¡Espero que todavía les interese estudiar español después de terminar este capítulo! 19. Las noticias me interesarán. 20. ¡(A ella) le gusto!

14 Comparisons

14·1 1. Tú eres más alto que Tomás. 2. Mi hermano corre tan rápido como ellos. 3. Su hermana tiene tanto dinero como yo. 4. Hoy hace menos frío que ayer. 5. Llueve más aquí que en Arizona. 6. El Sr. Acero es tan malo como el diablo. 7. Juana es la alumna más lista de la clase. 8. Hay menos de cinco libros en la mesa. 9. ¡Los padres siempre son mayores que sus hijos! 10. Pedro es el químico más preparado del equipo. 11. María y Teresa bailan mejor que yo. 12. Estos dos son los peores platos del menú. 13. Me gusta este postre más que el otro. 14. ¡Es un jugador de baloncesto altísimo! 15. Juanito tiene tantos juguetes como su hermanita. 16. Hay menos nieve en esta montaña que en la otra. 17. Este carro es más costoso que el otro. 18. Ella lee tantas revistas como yo. 19. Esa muchacha es la más interesante de todas. 20. La oveja no bebe tanta agua como el camello.

14·2 1. The children didn't sleep as many hours as I did. 2. My girlfriend has hair as long as her mother. / My girlfriend's hair is as long as her mother's. 3. That girl is drop-dead gorgeous. 4. Are you as popular as he is? 5. Do you have as many friends as I do?

6. I don't believe (that) John is younger than you are. 7. What's your oldest sibling's name? (sibling, *because it could be a brother or a sister*) 8. There are no more than five (*i.e., five, no more, no less*) on a basketball team. 9. She is as much of a crybaby as her aunt. 10. Which is the biggest country in the world? 11. Puerto Rico is not as big as Cuba. 12. New York doesn't have as many people as Mexico City. 13. There are fewer than four pizzas in the refrigerator. 14. You're as friendly as they told me. 15. George likes to play tennis as much as he does to watch movies. 16. I love to swim in the ocean more than in lakes. 17. These two are the most athletic ones in the group. 18. She doesn't have as much energy as we hoped. 19. On the table there are as many ballpoint pens as there are pencils. 20. More than anything, he was interested in making little gold fish.

14·3 1. ¿Quién es / será la persona más importante de tu vida? 2. ¿Qué quieren hacer sus amigos más que nada? 3. Ella es la mujer más rica del mundo. 4. ¿Tienen tantas camisas como calcetines / medias? 5. Ella es la mejor nadadora del equipo. 6. Ella pinta tanto como él. 7. No hay menos de mil libros en esta colección. 8. Su mamá vende más que yo. 9. ¿Cuál es el lago más profundo de los Estados Unidos? 10. El Atlántico es más pequeño que el Pacífico. 11. Su hermano es más joven que tú. 12. No somos los jugadores más altos del equipo. 13. Este reloj cuesta tanto como ése / aquél. 14. ¿Quién tiene / tendrá tantos zapatos como ella? 15. Somos los mejores cocineros del pueblo. 16. Venus puede brillar tanto como el foco de un avión. 17. Hay más peces en este lago que en ése / aquél. 18. Él es el peor jugador de ajedrez de la escuela. 19. Él va al cine tanto como yo. 20. Ella escribe tan bien como canta.

15 Indefinite words

15·1 1. k 2. d 3. h 4. a 5. c 6. i 7. b 8. j 9. e 10. g 11. l 12. f

15·2 1. b 2. a 3. b 4. c 5. c 6. a 7. b 8. c 9. a 10. c 11. c 12. b 13. b 14. c 15. b 16. c 17. c 18. b 19. c 20. b

15·3 1. ¿Hay alguien aquí que me pueda ayudar? 2. No quiero comer pizza tampoco. / Tampoco quiero comer pizza. 3. No hay galleta alguna en la bandeja. 4. ¿Tienen algún vino que sea muy bueno? 5. El café no se preparaba a tiempo nunca. / Nunca se preparaba el café a tiempo. (**jamás** *is also admissible*) 6. Alguien llamó por ti esta mañana. 7. No conozco a nadie que haya escalado esa montaña. 8. No hay nadie que haya escalado esa montaña. / Nadie ha escalado esa montaña. 9. ¡Cualquier médico te lo puede decir! 10. Algún vendedor te dejó esta muestra. 11. No hay nadie en esta clase que lea más que yo. / Nadie en esta clase lee más que yo.   12. Leo más que nadie en esta clase.   13. Cualquiera que crea al Sr. Acero, está loco.   14. No conozco a nadie que lo pueda hacer tampoco. / A nadie conozco que lo pueda hacer tampoco.   15. No está / hay nadie en casa. / Nadie está / hay en casa.   16. (A él) le gusta montar en bicicleta también.   17. No iban nunca a ese restaurante. / Nunca iban a ese restaurante. 18. Hay algo / Algo hay que la molesta.   19. No fue nada, un regalito nada más.   20. ¡¿No vas nunca a la playa?! / ¡¿Nunca vas a la playa?!

16   Relative pronouns

16·1   1. Veo al hombre que compró un auto ayer.   2. ¿Conoces a las chicas a quienes les diste unos dulces? 3. El Sr. Acero mintió, lo cual le va a causar muchos problemas.   4. Hablé con tu hermano, para quien hice un favor.   5. Acabo de ver de nuevo a Teresa, con quien fui al cine la semana pasada. 6. Los niños juegan al escondite, que / el cual es un juego muy popular.   7. ¿Viste a ese policía que me puso una multa?   8. Voy a llamar a las tres chicas que salieron de clase temprano.   9. Conozco bien a Tomás, de quien te hablé mucho anoche.   10. Leyeron las noticias de ayer, las cuales no les gustaron. 11. Tengo un perro que sabe muchos trucos.   12. Vamos a buscar al dependiente que te ofreció un descuento anoche.   13. Subimos una escalera, que / la cual no está bien iluminada.   14. Ellos compraron la casa que tiene un patio amplio.   15. Vi a una de las hijas de la Sra. Gómez, que / la que tiene el pelo liso.   16. ¿Quieres acompañarme al parque que tiene columpios?   17. Juan vendió la heladería en la cual no manejaban paletas.   18. ¿Compraste el pastel que tenía cerezas encima? 19. ¿Viste el gato que tenía un ojo verde y el otro amarillo?   20. Tienes una computadora que funciona bien.

16·2   1. No conozco al hombre de quien habla Ud.   2. Ella me trajo / llevó sopa, lo cual me agradó. 3. Vendimos el carro que no funcionaba bien.   4. Ellos llamaron al hijo del Sr. González, que / quien es médico.   5. ¿Viste el partido de que él escribió en el periódico?   6. De los tres muchachos que corrían, el que / quien se cayó es mi hermano menor.   7. Sus tres perros grandes, que ganaron el concurso, todos tienen cuatro años.   8. Él fue al cine, aunque no tenía quién lo acompañara.   9. La caja que trajo estaba vacía.   10. El hombre a quien yo vi era alto y llevaba un traje gris.   11. El gerente cuya tienda se cerró decidió renunciar a su cargo.   12. La mujer de quien recibí un mensaje no volvió a llamarme. 13. Su mamá, que / quien es de Francia, me trajo una botella de vino.   14. Entrevistamos a cinco postulantes, entre los cuales sólo uno era bilingüe.   15. Sus hermanas que fueron a ver la película volvieron a casa temprano.   16. A sus amigos, que / quienes habían leído la novela, les gustó mucho el club de libros.   17. Los que me gustaban / me caían bien, los invité al concierto.   18. El vino, que estaba en cajas, se envió al restaurante.   19. ¿Conoces al hombre cuya esposa es presidente de su propia compañía?   20. Vimos a la mujer de quien recibimos el regalo.

17   Subordinated clauses

17·1   1. It was doubtful (that) my cousins had prepared dinner when my father arrived.   2. I think it is possible that it will rain tomorrow. (*The verb* **llover** *is governed by the notion of possibility, while the verb* **ser** *is governed by a verb of belief.*)   3. We were looking for a shotgun that had two barrels.   4. My father had a garden that produced / used to produce a lot of tomatoes.   5. When you decide if you're going to go with me or not, you'll call me, won't you?   6. He / She / You will sell the car provided at least five hundred dollars is offered (to him / her / you).   7. The children hope (that) we'll all play soccer.   8. It is essential that you and I come to an agreement.   9. The three of them wanted me to stay home until it quit raining. 10. It's odd that she always has insisted that I not call her on weekends. (*There are two subordinated clauses, both governed by verbs that make the subjunctive necessary.*)   11. No matter how much we asked him to lend us the money, he refused to lend it to us.   12. We need a program that will allow us to process more data in less time.   13. She has a boyfriend who loves her a lot.   14. We doubt (that) Henry's parents have forgotten his birthday.   15. They are glad that you haven't abandoned your studies.   16. I ask that you call me before the market closes. (**rogar** *is a very polite verb for asking, corresponding to the formal, and now seldom encountered, use of* to beg)   17. Do you want me to find a movie that isn't a horror film? 18. After he bathed, John got dressed and took off (left).   19. Before he left the house, John bathed and got dressed.   20. It's impossible (that) she didn't find out about it before the party. (*or* know about it)

17·2   1. Su mamá se alegra de que tú hayas visto el drama.   2. Fuimos a la tienda antes de que nuestro papá viniera / regresara / llegara a casa.   3. ¿Quieres que te lea el cuento?   4. Ella y yo tuvimos que buscar un carro que tuviera un reproductor de CDs.   5. ¿Te preocupas de que la computadora no tenga suficiente memoria?   6. ¿Les pidieron que trajeran el informe?   7. Tuvieron que hallar una farmacia que

estuviera / permaneciera abierta las veinticuatro horas.   8. Sabemos que le has escrito las cartas.
9. Están seguros de que él había visto la película antes de que su mamá regresara / volviera a casa.
10. Fue importante que él terminara la carrera.   11. Es dudoso que Catherine haya publicado o que
publique un artículo.   12. Ella les exigía a sus alumnos que tuvieran escritas cinco páginas al final de cada
semana.   13. Fue un milagro que él no se hubiera ahogado.   14. Fue obvio que su mamá no hubiera
querido / deseado que ella viniera a nuestra fiesta.   15. Ellos nos prometieron que nos ayudarían, con
tal de que les pagáramos por adelantado.   16. Si tú me pidieras que te hiciera un favor, te lo haría.
17. Después de que Uds. se hayan desayunado, podemos ir al zoológico.   18. ¡Es bueno / Qué bueno
que vayas al concierto!   19. Ella entró en la casa de nuevo sin que sus padres lo supieran.   20. Vimos al
vendedor que nos vendió el carro.

18 Pero, sino, sino que, and other sentence-building devices

18·1   1. pero   2. sino   3. sino que   4. sino   5. sino   6. sino que   7. sino   8. pero   9. sino que
10. sino que   11. sino que   12. pero   13. sino   14. pero   15. pero   16. sino   17. sino que
18. pero   19. sino que   20. pero

18·2   1. Queremos trabajar en el jardín pero llueve / está lloviendo.   2. Él no tiene una computadora, sino una
máquina de escribir.   3. No tomamos / estamos tomando café, sino té.   4. ¡Mis amigos no trabajaban,
sino que dormían!   5. ¡Fue a pescar, pero no pescó ni un pez!   6. Ella no quiso preparar la cena, sino
mirar una película y pedir una pizza.   7. Ni María ni Juan fueron a la fiesta.   8. Cuanto más escucho
la música clásica, tanto más me gusta.   9. Ella no sólo leyó el periódico, sino todas las revistas también.
10. Mañana o va a llover / lloverá o va a nevar / nevará.   11. Cuanto menos él leía, tanto más tonto
les parecía a los demás.   12. No es oro, sino plata.   13. La luna no es de queso, pero es amarillo.
14. Ella vivió en Panamá desde 1990 hasta 2000.   15. Mis amigos y yo cocinamos tanto como comemos.
16. Él no le llamó (a ella), sino que le escribió una carta.   17. Hoy en día / actualmente, la gente no
escribe cartas, sino que todos se mandan / envían mensajes de texto.   18. Daniel no entró por la puerta
de enfrente sino por la de atrás.   19. Él o va a volar / volará o va a tomar / tomará un tren a Montevideo. /
Él irá a Montivideo o en / por avión o en / por tren.   20. Yo no quiero ni huevos ni tocino.

19 Calendar dates, time, and phone numbers

19·1   1. l.   2. d.   3. i.   4. a.   5. g.   6. j.   7. k.   8. e.   9. f.   10. h.   11. b.   12. c.

19·2   1. El sábado, doce de marzo del año dos mil once, terminé de escribir este libro.   2. El partido de fútbol
comenzó a la una y quince / cuarto de la tarde, el sábado, ocho de enero del año dos mil once.   3. El año
pasado, el primero de marzo fue un lunes.   4. Para las cuatro de la tarde hoy, habré trabajado diez horas.
5. El lunes, tengo una cita a las tres de la tarde.   6. ¿A qué hora empezó la película?   7. Él vivió en la
Calle Ocho Norte, en el número tres cero cinco, desde junio del año mil novecientos setenta y ocho hasta
agosto del año mil novecientos ochenta.   8. No te olvides de llamarme una noche de éstas al dos treinta y
cinco, once cero dos.   9. En los países de habla española, los martes trece, no los viernes, se consideran
días de mala suerte.   10. ¿Sabe Ud. lo que / qué pasó el viernes, doce de octubre del año mil cuatrocientos
noventa y dos?   11. La Casa Blanca se ubica en la Avenida Pennsylvania, en el número mil seiscientos.
12. Creo que su número de ella es dos cuarenta y siete, noventa y cinco, treinta y ocho, pero no le llame los
domingos.   13. Ella nació el veintidós de enero del año mil novecientos noventa y ocho a las nueve y
cuarenta y cuatro de la mañana. Fue un jueves.   14. El veintidós de noviembre del año mil novecientos
sesenta y tres, fue un viernes.   15. Son las doce y uno de la mañana.   16. Los jueves, me acuesto a
la una menos quince / cuarto de la mañana, ¡lo que quiere decir que los miércoles no me acuesto!
17. La biblioteca se ubica en la Avenida Cuatro. A partir de marzo, se abre a las nueve de la mañana todos
los días, excepto los domingos.   18. Son las veintidós y cuarenta y cinco.   19. *Answers will vary, but
the formats are in this chapter and in this answer key.*   20. *Answers will vary.*

20 Numbers, math, and statistics

20·1   1. k.   2. s.   3. q.   4. h.   5. m.   6. o.   7. l.   8. b.   9. r.   10. a.   11. d.   12. i.   13. f.
14. c.   15. t.   16. e.17. p.   18. j.   19. n.   20. g.

20·2   1. tres y / más cinco son ocho   2. cuarenta y dos (multiplicado) por treinta y cuatro son mil cuatrocientos
veintiocho   3. ochenta y nueve dividido por siete son doce con cinco restantes / y quedan (*or* restan) cinco.

4. setenta y siete menos cincuenta y dos son veinticinco   5. noventa y tres (multiplicado) por siete son seiscientos cincuenta y uno   6. dos tercios / dos terceras partes   7. dos séptimos / dos séptimas partes 8. tres cuartos / tres cuartas partes   9. un medio   10. cuatro quintos / cuatro quintas partes 11. tres cuartos / cuartas partes más / y un medio igual a uno y cuarto / una cuarta parte *(using* **igual a** *avoids the potencial confusion even native speakers of Spanish can feel when faced with whether to use* **es** *or* **son** *when the result is one* plus *a fraction)*   12. cinco coma tres menos cuatro coma uno igual a uno coma dos (or use **punto** instead of **coma**, depending on notation system of the country).   13. seis menos cinco es uno   14. el noventa y siete por ciento   15. ciento y uno menos uno son cien   16. diez (multiplicado) por cien son mil (**un** *is not used before* **mil**)   17. mil más uno son mil y uno / mil y uno son mil y uno 18. setecientos setenta y siete más / y quinientos cincuenta y cinco son mil trescientos treinta y dos 19. tres séptimos / tres séptimas partes   20. el veintitrés por ciento

20·3   1. It is believed that the bear market will continue unless the Reserve takes measures.   2. It has been calculated that the death rate from the bubonic plague was 30% of the population.   3. The secretary showed me a pamphlet with a bar graph.   4. The stock broker has a call option that expires at close of business.   5. The economy's growth rate has slowed due to civil wars in the region.   6. The initiation fee is $187 and thereafter it is $140 per year.   7. The board of directors announced that it will reinvest 5% of profits in publicity campaigns.   8. The amount dedicated to education is 4% less this year compared to last year.   9. One study of economic conditions revealed that there is a range of possibilities for resolving the crisis.   10. The creditors have proposed an increase in interest rates of 4%.   11. For a week, the price of the stock fluctuated between $40 and $50.   12. Congress approved a 2% increase on imported consumer goods.   13. In order to show their opposition to the anti-union sentiments of the governor, the workers went on strike.   14. The personnel in charge of research and development received a salary increase of 4%. 15. Due to the fact that the inflation rate is at 9% per year and that the unemployment rate is approaching 12%, it is doubtful that the ruling party is going to remain in control after the coming elections, whether in the legislative bodies or in executive positions.

CPSIA information can be obtained
at www.ICGtesting.com
Printed in the USA
BVHW010929031120
592249BV00013B/83

9 780071 756198